Pagan Portals

The Inner-City Path

A Simple Guide to Well-Being and Awareness

Pagan Portals

The Inner-City Path

A Simple Guide to Well-Being and Awareness

Mélusine Draco

MOON
BOOKS

Winchester, UK
Washington, USA

JOHN HUNT PUBLISHING

First published by Moon Books, 2020
Moon Books is an imprint of John Hunt Publishing Ltd., No. 3 East Street, Alresford
Hampshire SO24 9EE, UK
office@jhpbooks.net
www.johnhuntpublishing.com
www.moon-books.net

For distributor details and how to order please visit the 'Ordering' section on our website.

ISBN: 978 1 78904 464 5
978 1 78904 465 2 (ebook)
Library of Congress Control Number: 2019948227

A CIP catalogue record for this book is available from the British Library.

Design: Stuart Davies

UK: Printed and bound by CPI Group (UK) Ltd, Croydon, CR0 4YY
US: Printed and bound by Thomson-Shore, 7300 West Joy Road, Dexter, MI 48130

We operate a distinctive and ethical publishing philosophy in
all areas of our business, from our global network of authors to
production and worldwide distribution.

Contents

Dedicated to Elen Sentier
... one who has the gift

A Gleaning of the Seasons

The (Inner-City) Path: A Gleaning of the Seasons was inspired by Chet Raymo's book of similar title that chronicled his own daily urban walk to work and observing the seasonal changes with a scientist's curiosity. As often happens, I began thinking 'what if' there was a complementary book written from a pagan perspective for when we take to our local urban paths as part of our daily fitness regime or dog walk. And, as if arising from this external creative impulse *The Path* began to unravel in the mind's eye ... based on several urban walks that have merged together over the years to make a chapbook of the seasons and to offer a glimpse into the pagan mind-set that can 'find mystery under every leaf and rock along the way', or caught in the murmur of running water, and to act as a simple guide to achieving a sense of well-being and awareness so that *even in the city's throng we feel the freshness of the streams as per Longfellow's 'Prelude"* ...

Generally speaking, witches and pagans come in all shapes and sizes from baby-boomers to millennials and each one is a product of their own generation, complete with all its fads, quirks, foibles and urban myths. By and large, for an older witch, a sense of well-being and awareness focuses on a need for inner harmony and being at peace with what they've achieved thus far in life, while looking forward to whatever challenges the future throws at them. For the younger variety, their sense of well-being and awareness is often preaching the gospel via social media (in all its many forms and contradictions) that has frequently made them appear less tolerant, more judgemental, and possibly a tad too obsessed with bodily functions. We are *all* a product of our Age ... *all* as different as Nature intended ... even town and city dwellers may have unconscious pagan leanings.

Nevertheless, we also know that Mother Nature is neither

caring nor motherly and when she wants to cut up rough – she will, without a thought for anything, or anyone. In the guise of 'the goddess' she is usually seen as spending her days caring for her many children who inhabit and shape the landscape – often portrayed in trailing garments composed of lush plants, colorful flowers, and sinuous woody shapes. In most depictions she is meditative, embodying the spirit of the mythological 'mother' in Nature. In reality, humankind and nature can be said to be in *conflict*, since Nature is often seen by humans as natural resources to be exploited; while Nature will wipe out hundreds of humans with a shrug of the shoulder.

Getting back to Nature requires stripping away the anthropomorphism that causes us to interpret non-human things in terms of human characteristics. Derived from the Greek *anthropos* (meaning 'human') and morphe ('form'), the term was first used to refer to the attribution of human physical or mental features to deities. According to *Britannica*, by the mid-19th century it had acquired the second, broader meaning of a phenomenon occurring not only in religion but in all areas of human thought and action, including daily life, the arts, and even sciences. Anthropomorphism may occur consciously or unconsciously and most scholars since the time of the English philosopher Francis Bacon (1561–1626) have agreed that although the tendency to anthropomorphise hinders the understanding of the world, it *is* deep-seated and persistent. But is it so wrong to consider *all* living, growing things as sentient beings?

The Path we regularly take when out for a daily walk has its own welcoming ambiance and if we feel as though we're being swamped with negative emotions, we know it can be helpful to walk them off. In fact, a recent British health study showed that simply walking in green spaces induces a gentle state of meditation. Most of us live in urban areas and spend far less time outside in green, natural spaces than people did several generations ago but even a lunchtime stroll in the park may soothe the mind and, in the process, change the workings of our brain in ways that improve our mental health. Whatever the weather, walking in Nature is not only good for our heart and fitness levels, but according to numerous studies it has measurable mental benefits and may also reduce the risk of depression. In addition to promoting mental health, nature group walks also 'appear to mitigate the effects of stressful life events on perceived stress and negative affects while synergizing with physical activity to improve positive affects and mental well-being', the researchers wrote in the Researchgate study abstract.

'Wellness' entered the pagan lexicon with the advent of Mind, Body & Spirit magazine publishing in the 1980s when it was generally used to mean 'a state beyond the absence of illness' and aimed at promoting a sense of well-being. It quickly became an umbrella term for pseudo-scientific mumbo-jumbo and alternative health movements - becoming the defining spirit or mood of the 2000s as reflected by the ideas and beliefs of the time. All of which promoted journalist Hadley Freeman to write in the *Guardian* as early as 2015: 'Pseudoscience and strawberries: 'wellness' gurus should carry a health warning'.

It's easy to mock wellness bloggers and their fattening apples, but their uneducated bletherings about food and health are, at best, irresponsible and, at heart, immoral. They're right: what we eat is important, which is why it's important that people with qualifications beyond an Instagram account educate us about it.

Nevertheless, a considerable amount of traditional witchcraft/ paganism revolves around natural folk-cures and herbal remedies, with much of it having been handed down by grandparents and elderly neighbours in rural communities. Foraging was part of growing up and knowing when and where in the country calendar certain delicacies could be found; and who, as a rural child experienced the bliss of gorging themselves on wild, woodland strawberries, has ever forgotten that exquisite taste? Or returning home with fingers and mouths stained purple from picking blackberries by the bushel as part of a school-dinners project?

'Awareness' is an even more recent innovation commonly used in reference to public knowledge or understanding of social or political issues. It is synonymous with public involvement and advocacy in support of certain causes or movements; or concern about and a well-informed interest in a particular situation or development. Awareness in the spiritual sense is harder to describe in intellectual terms but on a basic level it can refer to a mental state achieved by focusing our awareness on the present moment, while calmly acknowledging and accepting our feelings, thoughts, and bodily sensations ... Awareness can mean different things and the first steps we can take on the pagan path is to become aware of the everyday world of Nature that surrounds us ... *even in the city's throng* ...

Several decades ago, it was agreed that if it was to survive, witchcraft *had* to move with the times and although there was a romantic appeal in returning to the Old Ways, it was not always practical. In the years since the repeal of the Witchcraft Act in 1951, the Craft *has* evolved in many separate ways and when something evolves, it changes, or develops over time and much can be lost in the process: like our taste in music and literature, which transforms as we get older, and generally changes from one generation to the next. And yet ... some things never change.

American photographer Frances F. Denny attempted to explore the figure of the contemporary witch beyond the cultural chestnuts that have shrouded and obscured it for *Elle* magazine:

The muddled stereotypes that surround witches nowadays are, in the end, not so very different from those used to define that perennial problem: woman. Her subjects are of diverse age, social class, and ethnicity, and practice a range of rituals, often drawing on 'mysticism, engagement with the occult, politically oriented activism, polytheism, ritualized 'spell-work' and plant-based healing.

Denny asked the women she photographed for the series to wear an outfit or bring along an item that they felt would represent their practice and identity as witches, and as a result:

> ...some of the portraits do answer more readily to our expectations of what a witch might look like. They brandish mysterious implements - a crystal ball, a bow and arrow, a wooden staff; one woman reclines, entwined with a snake - and most are dressed in black. There was an immense theatricality...

Nevertheless, the 'witch' has firmly entered the 21st-century zeitgeist as a figure akin to a synergetic composite of Burne-Jones in the terminal stages of the Pre-Raphaelite movement, Guinevere, of Arthurian romance, and Daenerys Stormborn from *Game of Thrones* – reflecting the general intellectual, moral, and cultural climate of the era. All of which appears to be an out-and-out attempt to make a statement and stand out from the crowd when our forebears would have done everything in their power to blend in with their neighbours! But it's not always like that ... since many traditional witches have learned the art of blending in.

Within esoteric circles the term 'path' is often used to refer to the *spiritual* journey that many of us take as part of our esoteric learning. In this book *The Path* is a series of gentle mental exercises to limber up the 'spiritual vagabond' part of our make-up *before* we embark on a much more challenging adventure as we metamorphose from embryonic pagan to fully-fledged witch. It helps if we get into a mind-set that plays a critical role in how we cope with life's new challenges regardless of age or background and imbues us with a hunger for learning about the natural world around us. A pagan mindset is also about living up to our possible potential and who knows how far we can go if we set our mind to it - believing that the effort that goes into learning and deepening our understanding is well worth all the toil and trouble as we chart our way through the seasons.

For example: most of us overlook a bountiful food supply, one that satisfies us personally and, in a very small way, may benefit us financially: the wild larder. We have become so out of touch with food that we no longer recognize wild ingredients as something we can utilize for sheer enjoyment. Foraging puts us back in touch with nature and introduces us to new tastes we can use creatively. Gathering wild leaves and fruits is not the sole preserve of the country dweller as even a touch of wild garlic can enhance urban cooking.

It now becomes obvious why 'gleaning' was chosen as part of the title for *The (Inner-City) Path: A Gleaning of the Seasons* because it means to collect information in small amounts and often with difficulty. The conditions of farm workers in the 1890s made gleaning essential because it was the act of collecting leftover crops from farmers' fields after they have been commercially harvested, or on fields where it was not economically profitable to harvest. In other words, we are picking up bits and pieces of information to add to our meager store of knowledge in order to supplement our life-style and its modern links with the natural world. And *A Simple Guide to Well-Being & Awareness* ... well, as Dryden wrote: '*what* herbs and Simples grow. In fields and *forests, all their powers I know*' when referring to using a single herb or plant in a medicinal way.

And it is at this point we step out onto **The Path** ... and a return to a pagan sense of well-being and awareness ... and a feeling of wonder in everyday life.

Chapter One

Getting Out there

There *is* power in Nature. A law unto herself and uncontrollable, nevertheless, Nature does offer a healing respite from the hustle and bustle of daily life. No cramped offices, no traffic, no emails, no mobile phones – even a municipal park bench is a stark departure from what modern society tends to consider important. Throughout the ages, spiritually-inclined men and women have understood the power of Nature, using the wilderness to cultivate an inner spirituality that in turn makes a meaningful impact on the lives of others. It is in this wilderness of the soul, stripped of distraction, that we face ourselves and our circumstances in one of the rawest and most vulnerable ways we'll ever experience.

Pause for a moment and think about the last time *you* incorporated a practice solely for the sake of your spiritual life. If you can't remember, it's probably time you allocated time in your busy schedule for yourself. This 'time' won't create itself; you will need to make it a priority. Unlike physical health, which often takes precedence with exercise and healthy eating, spiritual well-being is a little more elusive and is, more often than not, put on the back-burner. As *Leisure* by Welsh poet W. H. Davies reminds us …

What is this life if, full of care,
We have no time to stand and stare.
No time to stand beneath the boughs
And stare as long as sheep or cows.
No time to see, when woods we pass,
Where squirrels hide their nuts in grass.
No time to see, in broad daylight,

Streams full of stars, like skies at night.
No time to turn at Beauty's glance,
And watch her feet, how they can dance.
No time to wait till her mouth can
Enrich that smile her eyes began.
A poor life this if, full of care,
We have no time to stand and stare.

In traditional British Old Craft, we put spiritual health at the *top* of our list and make a point of spending time contemplating Nature – even if it's only *five minutes* a day while we drink a cup of coffee in the garden watching birds and listening to bees. That's our very own five minutes during which nothing and no one is allowed to intrude. This is important 'me-time' and it's amazing just how much we can absorb in those few precious moments. The iridescent colours in a magpie's feathers; a spider's web glittering with dew; a scattering of droplets in the grass after a shower; the murmur of a breeze among the leaves; the scent of freshly cut grass ... all in themselves magical moments that we don't usually take time to notice. Although in the 12th-century St Anselm did consider it spiritually dangerous to sit in a garden because it was so pleasant to the senses!

By following **The Path,** we will learn to explore those hidden spaces that we have passed a hundred times without noticing what kind of plants grow in urban gardens, or by the side of the verge, or bothered to identify the trees in the woods that go through their annual cycle, year after year. We need to understand that on a *daily* basis we are living near a portal between knowledge and mystery; between the commonplace and the divine. And during those brief five minutes each day we are standing on the threshold of that portal, poised one day to step through and discover all that knowledge and mystery for ourselves.

Hedgerows and field margins, boundaries of the park and

woodland rides, alleys and backstreets of a market town, or the tow-path of the canal and river walks will often offer up unexpected liminal experiences where we have the sensation of stepping through some invisible barrier. A liminal space is the time between the 'what was' and the 'next'. It is a place of transition, of waiting, and not knowing. Liminal spaces are where all transformation takes place, if we learn how to wait and let it inform us. Author and theologian Richard Rohr describes this condition as:

> Where we are betwixt and between the familiar and the completely unknown. There alone is our old world left behind, while we are not yet sure of the new existence. That's a good space where genuine newness can begin. Get there often and stay as long as you can by whatever means possible ... This is the sacred space where the old world is able to fall apart, and a bigger world is revealed ... Change never exists in a box, no matter how hard we might try to contain it. Change in one area of life always spills into others that disrupt the status quo. There is a ripple effect. Community, spirituality, vocation, relationships, physicality, friendships and emotions do not exist mutually exclusive from one another - they intersect and intertwine. When we become aware of our own liminality, most of us, if we're honest, don't know who to become or how to navigate the transition. We often miss the real potential of 'in-between' places – we either stand paralyzed or we flee the 'terrible cloud of unknown' instead of confidently moving forward into our future.

Unfortunately, there is something in our modern nature and/or culture (especially in the West) that has conditioned us to want the easy path. We want to get to the 'spiritual' without making the long journey with a competent guide; we yearn for those non-existent tools and practices that will help us avoid the darkness, not to mention the uncertainty and a fear of this unknown. And as a result, we steer clear of those thresholds and portals that are part and parcel of normal spiritual growth.

Nevertheless, most of us generally walk the same path time and time again: along by the old church yard and cottage gardens, through urban woodland and across fields, passed old orchards and allotments, across streams and along the tow-path or river bank. We have walked that path so many times, we could navigate it blindfold even at dawn and dusk. We know the landscape so well that we can anticipate when the first dog violets and wild primroses will be in bloom by the hedge. We know the moments of sunrise and sunset, the phases of the moon, and when Orion will appear in the East. This is an awareness that is often bred in the bone and yet for all its familiarity not a day goes by when we walk **The Path** *without* seeing something of note.

As American Chet Raymo observed when writing *The Path: A One-Mile Walk Through the Universe,* every pebble and wildflower has a story to tell. A flake of granite in the tarmac was once at the core of towering mountains pushed up when continents collided:

> The purple loosestrife beside the stream emigrated from Europe in the 1800s as a garden ornamental, then went wantonly native in a land of wild frontiers ... Scratch a name in a landscape, and history bubbles up like a spring.

It should not be thought, however, that witches spring fully informed about the natural world, but for every book on their shelves relating to magic and spell-craft, there will probably be a dozen referring to native flora and fauna. And for a witch the very word 'path' has many different connotations in the esoteric sense because when we talk of a pagan path, it conjures up a spiritual, magical or mystical journey. Outwardly, we can see many differences but it would be a mistake to give too much importance to those outer forms. True spirituality depends on our *inner* attitude, our inner belief and sincerity and - whichever path we follow - we need follow it with devotion, sincerity and humility. It is only when we actively pursue a spiritual path with integrity and fidelity that belief can become a true spiritual experience rather than just a collection of well-worn platitudes learned from the internet.

The Path is designed to re-focus the mind on the power of the natural world in order to follow the way we have chosen to take on a *daily basis* – whether we walk past a ruined church yard or modest urban gardens we still encounter the changing seasons if we have a mind to look. Every day going to and from school we walked along a narrow jitty by the remains of the medieval church tower and churchyard of St Mary Magdalen that had been destroyed in the fire of 1742. The overgrown churchyard in the centre of town with its somber evergreens was surrounded by high limestone walls and an iron fence that confined the four scary gargoyles leering down from the tower ... but it also contained a wealth of ivy-covered gravestones swathed in enormous bouquets of creamy-white cow parsley and the enclosing walls festooned with delicate ivy-leaved toadflax. It was always a magical place that I can still see in my mind's eye even though the conservationists have – between then and now - ruined it beyond measure. It was from that dark, distressed environment came the introduction to wild plants of a poisonous nature like the celandine, foxglove and dog's mercury ... and the members of the wonderful nightshade family.

By contrast the small market-town back gardens offered a cornucopia of brightly jewelled flowers, ornamental shrubs and neat clipped lawns viewed through gaps in the fences to the accompaniment of kitchen radios. Next to the Nature-controlled darkness of the churchyard, the gardens were always a riot of spring bulbs and summer planting, autumn colour and winter neatness. The wild side of Nature was never allowed to intrude into these havens of light, and peace, and orderliness - but there was always the reminder that darkness was never far away.

Not far from those tidy, well-kept gardens we find ourselves following *The Path* through the small patch of urban woodland heading towards the field beyond. This is a scruffy wood, mostly oaks and birches and *The Path* is confined to well-worn tracks, three or four feet wide that are kept open by villagers or townspeople regularly walking their dogs. Beside *The Path* sunlight falls on swathes of dog's mercury and the long, spear-shaped leaves of the bluebells – for this is an *old* wood, here long before the village was extended around it. The open field is a fifteen-acre site of 'specific scientific interest' and one of the best examples of 'poorly drained grassland, dominated by tufted hair-grass and typical meadow species as saw-wort, meadow thistle, knapweed and lady's smock'.

From the place where a plank bridge crosses the stream by a rowdy duck pond, *The Path* takes us between allotments and old orchards – with just a few gnarled trees still standing - and passed a broad, low-lying water meadow that floods in winter, or after a particularly heavy summer rainfall. Sometimes *The Path* itself floods and as Chet Raymo observes:

> Only an immersion in nature will give us the requisite wisdom. I stand by the side of the water meadow ... and feel the tug of billions of generations of plants rooting me in mystery, in the foundational muck of the meadow, in the teeming dark abyss of time.

In spring, one by one the gardeners appear on the individual plots of the allotments, with their packets of seeds and seedlings - and in the summer and autumn they harvest. Many would consider this a pointless exercise since it is possible to buy vegetables from the supermarket for less money than the cost of a packet of seeds ... but that is not the point of the exercise because as Chet Raymo observes 'What's really going on is a love affair with seeds, with the soil and the sweet tactile sensation of snapping a homegrown sugar-pea or holding a hefty fresh tomato in the hand'.

If time is plentiful, the path can take us along the tow-path or river bank in the shade of the willows and where, in summer, adders could once be seen basking in the sun. Passed the old Barley Mow bathing place where the village children learned to swim, and along the bank where the river runs slow and deep with rushes and tendrils of waterweed waving in the current ...

Where the pools are bright and deep,
Where the grey trout lies asleep,
Up the river and over the lea,
That's the way for Billy and me ...
[*Boy's Song,* James Hogg]

Water was sacred to all ancient cultures and every pool and stream was believed to have its resident spirit. Here we stop and reflect that most of this water gravitates back to the oceans in a ceaseless cycle that has been in motion for four-billion years 'in trickle and torrent, eroding and shaping the land, and our local brook is only a tiny conduit in this unceasing flow'.

Our path eventually brings us back into the teeming everyday world but for those few magical steps we have left 'today' behind to learn the language and communicate with Nature throughout the seasons of the year. And the more adept we become at learning this language the more we come to understand that if we walked this same path every day for the rest of our lives, it will never be the same two days running. Each day will stimulate and heighten our senses to such a pitch as to become almost painful in the possessing.

Sight is the faculty or power of 'seeing' and the ability to interpret the surrounding environment using light in the visible spectrum reflected by the objects in the environment. This is different from 'visual acuity', which refers to how clearly a person sees (for example '20/20 vision'). The sight in animals allows them to assimilate information from their surroundings but a human can often have a problem with 'seeing' even if they do have 20/20 vision. 'Seeing' within the pagan mind means having the ability to observe everything in the natural world from many different levels and perspectives.

Sound interprets vibrations that travel through the air or another medium and can be heard when they reach human or animal ears. As in the case of other senses, the hearing of the primitive had been found to be extraordinary keen, acuteness beyond anything known among so-called civilized peoples. Proverbs and folk-lore furnish a number of expressions relative to acuteness of hearing. In Norse mythology Heimdallr is so wise that he could hear the wool grow on the sheep and the grass grow in the fields. 'To hear the grass grow' is a proverbial phrase found in Frisian and other Teutonic dialects - also 'to hear the worms cough'. The Eskimo shamans were said to be quick-eared enough to hear the voices of the spirits beside the waters of Otherworld; while in the myth and folk-lore of primitive races the origin of music, song, and speech is often attributed to birds. Within Craft we often find that our primitive hearing becomes more acute when we learn to block out extraneous noise and tune-in to the fluting song of the robin, the chittering of swallows and the distinctive drone of the bumble-bee.

Smell: The sense of smell is closely linked with memory, probably more so than any of our other senses. Those with full olfactory functions may be able to think of smells that evoke particular memories: the scent of an orchard in blossom conjuring up recollections of a childhood picnic, the evocative scent of a bluebell wood, and the sensory perfume of hawthorn in bloom. This can often happen spontaneously, with a smell acting as a trigger in recalling a long-forgotten event or experience. For the attuned pagan, the natural smells of Nature provide a bouquet of sensation as we stroll along *The Path*.

Touch: is perhaps the most overlooked sense and every one of us receives tactile information about the world around us every second of the day. Our tactile sense delineates our boundaries; it indicates where we end and something else begins. Without the sense of touch, we would not sense this boundary, and we would not know where *we* stop being. Without a sense of touch, a natural witch would have no physical awareness of the satin-smoothness of the bark of the beech, the icy cold of fresh spring water, or the enveloping laziness of stretching out on a rock in the afternoon sun.

Taste: There is a common misperception that the word 'taste' refers to everything we experience when we eat or drink. This isn't actually true. As we all know, taste is a matter of ... taste ... but what is 'taste', exactly? In the narrower sense, we mean the 'sense of taste', i.e. direct perception on the tongue. The way in which we perceive this, however, results from a combination of our senses of smell, taste and touch. For me, on a warm day with the wind coming from the West and being funneled along the Glen, it is possible to literally taste the salt-tang of the sea on the air, blown in from the coast some 60 miles away.

The Path finally brings us round in a circle so that we return home by the woodland ride on the opposite side of the wood that forms part of an old bridle-way. We pass the ruin of the charcoal burner's cottage and the old hazel coppice enclosed by a ditch and a low stone wall that once kept the deer from nibbling the new shoots. From here we walk through a narrow jitty back into the housing estate and our walk is over for the day ... although there are still pleasurable sights to be seen in the front gardens along the way.

Exercise: A Sense of Well-Being

Well-being is a term that is used a lot nowadays, but despite is being the very thing we all desire, it is not something easily understood. Well-being is something sought by just about everyone, because it includes so many positive things — feeling happy, healthy, socially connected, and purposeful – and when we think positive, we tend to have greater emotional feeling of well-being.

Most of us would agree that being surrounded by Nature makes us feel 'comfortable', and this is the reason we experience a reduction in stress levels when we're on *The Path*. Although the simple act of walking in a forest might not seem extraordinary, the benefits that people experience during and after a forest walk really do exist. Make a point of going out into Nature this week and sit against a tree for a minimum of ten minutes. Breathe in and feel the energy of the tree refresh you. Nature is powerful … connect with her.

> Imagine taking a walk in the forest right now. You feel the earth and leaves under your feet, the snap of twigs. You listen to the birdsong and look up through the breaks in the canopy to the sky above, noticing how the light filters through to a point just further along the track … You breathe in deeply … You smell the distinct forest aromas: moss, sap, earth and wood … You take it all in. [*Shinrin-yoku*, Professor Yoshifumi Miyazaki]

Shinrin-yoku is the Japanese way of 'forest bathing' for health and relaxation. It is the practice of walking slowly through the woods and in no hurry. It is used in a similar way to 'sun-bathing' and 'sea-bathing'. We don't literally take a bath, but we do bathe in the environment of the woodland, using all our senses to experience Nature up close.

The practice of *shinrin-yoku* is based on walking through the forest at a gentle pace for two hours or more. Keeping your phone switched off allows time to soak up the environment around you and come into the here and now. The phrase *shikan shouyou* means 'nothing but wandering along', something we rarely get a chance to do, but which is very beneficial.

Professor Miyazaki believes that forest therapy and other natural therapies are the most practical way to reduce our stress levels and increase relaxation. At the end of the day, our bodies and minds are adapted to Nature, which can be a considerable help in reducing the strain on healthcare services all over the world by integrating 'forest bathing' into healthcare and education. In today's stressful society there is a growing interest in how stimulation from Nature can provide a little oasis of calm in our daily lives.

Chapter Two

Spring - the Path of New Beginnings

This year we had a double-whammy of astronomical action: the Vernal Equinox, which marks the beginning of spring, along with the final Supermoon of the year. The Equinox occurred at 5:58 p.m. and the full moon/Supermoon less than four hours later at 9:43 p.m.: the Equinox being the precise moment the sun's rays shine directly on the equator. It's one of two days out of the year – the other being the Autumnal Equinox in September – when the Earth's axis is tilted neither toward nor away from the sun, resulting in roughly twelve hours of daylight and twelve hours of darkness almost everywhere on Earth.

Meteorologists, who define the seasons differently, say spring begins on 1st March but as far as traditional witches are concerned, we work in harmony with the equinoxes and solstices just as our ancestors did, and not by any paper calendar. Of course, Nature pays no attention to any pre-set clock, natural or otherwise, and there is often freak weather at the beginning of the year with snowdrops in bloom in November and snow during the last week in March ...

The plants of the March woodlands and meadows, however, can cope with the temporary chill, for the winds, although cold doesn't have the desiccating dryness of February. Frost is still a problem to plants, and the first of the sheltered woodland species to raise their vulnerable flowers, risking the next generation of their kind, do so in order to get ahead in the seed-production cycle before the more vigorous plants of late spring develop in a welter of showy blooms, confusing the pollinating insects. [*The Country Book of the Year*]

Once we start to open our minds to the natural world, however, probably one of the first things we notice is the different sounds that birds make – reminding us that the origin of music, song, and even speech, itself, was often attributed to birds. The crow is considered very wise and intelligent and in various cultures they are seen as messengers; in Sicily any unexplained sixth-sense presentiment that comes true is said to be as a result of 'talking with the crows'.

The most enchanting time to listen for bird song is at dawn and dusk. The dawn chorus is one of the most magical experiences in Nature and we don't have to get out of bed to listen to it. It's uplifting, noisy and can be quite ethereal at times as a multitude of birds of different species all sing together in harmony as morning breaks and light begins to fill the sky. What's more, many birds that live in urban areas, with increased traffic noise, have begun to evolve higher-pitched songs than those that live in country environments so that potential rivals and mates can hear them more clearly, while light pollution in many cities has led to a longer daily singing period for some others. The repeated phrases of a song thrush are often noticeable at dusk as well as dawn – although few birds will singer later in the day.

The dusk chorus, however, is a much subtler affair that has been described as 'more chamber ensemble than symphony orchestra', but it is nonetheless a very magical time of the day. As the light begins to fade and flocks of birds fly home to roost, the individual songsters begin their eerie repertoire against the brilliant hues of a sunset. A robin's Pan-pipe fluting is wistful and dreamy and can often be heard at night in urban areas. While the shrill bark of a pheasant breaks through the stillness … Or as the *Guardian's* country diarist continued:

A quintet of collared doves and wood pigeons provide crooning backing vocals for two blackbirds, whose rich, throaty calls rise and fall in a mellow jazz duet. A song thrush cascades through its fluting, looping repertoire, while a chiffchaff chants its name and dunnocks tinkle tunelessly from the undergrowth.

According to the RSPB:

...the late winter's dawn chorus is more like a sing-along than a full-blown operatic burst of sweet notes as clear and powerful as any superstar tenor ... A whirr of flickering wings and the star performer emerges from the undergrowth to take centre stage on a bare elder sprig. Another short, sharp aria as delivered with gusto. The recognisable explosion of notes and the subtle tones of the voice delivering them with such clarity are unmistakable. **Dunnocks** are the garden's most understated birds, regularly overlooked for the perceived drabness of their colour scheme and never truly recognised for the sweetness and power of their vocalisations.

Although at first glance the dunnock may look like a sparrow it has a much slimmer build, and a much narrower pointed bill. On closer inspection we see it is an attractive little bird with its rich brown, black-streaked plumage, its grey head and breast and its pinky-orange legs. Young birds resemble adults, but are browner with bolder streaks of black or dark brown on the plumage that extend to the head and breast; at this stage they are sometimes confused with young robins. Quiet and unobtrusive, it is often seen on its own, creeping along the edge of a flower bed or near to a bush, moving with a rather nervous, shuffling gait, often flicking its wings as it goes.

One sunny spring day, two students were chatting on the sidewalk. A small, black bird landed on the sidewalk near them. It hopped to and fro and pecked at crumbs on the pavement. The girl said: "Look, a male blackbird." The other student was surprised: he'd never been much interested in birds and he thought it was pretty clever if someone could identify a particular bird just like that. And to be able to see that it was a male, too! That bordered on pure genius. The second student remarked on this, and now it was the first student's turn to be surprised.

"But it's easy!" she replied, explaining that you can recognise a male blackbird by its size, its black plumage and orange beak. In the ensuing conversation, she pointed out that many different species of bird inhabit towns and cities, and that it's easy enough to get to know them with a pocket bird guide.

This aroused the interest of the other student, and also made him think, "If she can do it, then maybe I can, too." Indeed, after watching birds and looking them up in a bird guide for a while, our novice birder could also recognise a male blackbird when he saw one. It wasn't so difficult after all; and it didn't take genius.

What does this example tell us? It certainly wouldn't have been the first time that the uninitiated student had seen a blackbird, as it is such a common bird. He must have seen them dozens of times before, yet the observations never entered his consciousness and he forgot about them. In the situation described above, he did not know what he was seeing. At most, he might have seen 'something flutter' or 'a bird'. When he was told that the bird was a blackbird, his interest was aroused and a whole new world, the world of birds, opened up before him. A world that, until then, he had never consciously seen before. [*Observing with the Twelve Senses*]

In the late spring, a walk by the pond might allow us to glimpse two shy birds, whose rare sighting has long played their part in our memories: The Kingfisher and the Heron.

Above the crinkled mirror surface of the water where the gnats dance is a brighter flash of blue against the sky. A kingfisher hovers to aim his dagger beak before diving, swift as an arrow, to pick a stickleback from beneath the water; then away to where his new-found mate sits cheeping, awaiting her wedding breakfast. The newly joined pair, their tryst sealed with a stickleback, speed across the meadow to the streamside and the hole in the sandbank which will be home for the glossy white clutch of eggs the hen will lay at the top of a two-foot tunnel. [*The Country Book of the Year*].

The heron, of course, has had a much more chequered career. For centuries the bird has played its part in English life; in the past it was the quarry for the royal falconers, for whom it was deemed the highest prize and the greatest test of their falcon's skill. As countryman Dennis Furnell points out, however, it has taken the heron millions of years to evolve as a master-fisherman and it is unreasonable for humans to expect them to ignore the colourful contents of a garden pond. 'Killing a heron for doing what comes naturally is as morally indefensible as putting up a bird table and then shooting away the blue tits when they come to feed.' Wild creatures have no moral judgement, they are not aware of 'ownership' – they are only aware of their need for food.

Herons cannot be mistaken for anything else. With a six-foot wingspan they have a fairly ancient lineage and first appeared in the fossil record in the Paleogene period; by seven million years ago birds closely resembling the modern form had appeared. In ancient Egypt, the bird-deity Bennu, associated with the sun, creation, and rebirth (i.e. the phoenix), was depicted as a heron in New Kingdom artwork. In ancient Rome, the heron was a bird of divination that gave an augury (sign of a coming event) by its call, like the raven, stork, and owl. Herons are known for their beauty and grace but reflect different meanings in different cultures. For example, if a bird lands on our house we will have good luck (although in Ireland the reverse is true) and if some of its plumage floats down – then we will have amazing luck!

Late winter and early spring are the best time to begin to learn to identify trees and plants along *The Path* and as the weather gets warmer, we become conscious that we are seeing a re-enactment of a series of events that have been happening over and over for millennia. The lengthening of the days brings the promise of spring and in the cold earth there are stirrings of life. One of the first plants to come to our notice is the subtle grey-green leaf of the Woodbine (or wild honeysuckle) as it pushes its way up towards the light in the hedgerow or woodland scrub before the leaf canopy begins to form. This deciduous woody climber twines around other shrubs, trees and bushes; from June to October it has distinctive creamy flowers which become pale yellow after pollination, often reddish outside, while in autumn the scarlet berries appear in the hedgerows in clusters. Nevertheless, the best time for walking the woodland path is in spring when there is little sunlight on the woodland floor.

The countryman's observation for this time of year is 'Beware the Blackthorn Winter'. This is because although the Blackthorn is in full bloom by now, its pale, softly fragrant blossoms are often matched by frost-whitened grass or snow-covered hills. The blackthorn flowers before its leaves grow, so we get a real contrast of white flower against black bark; blackthorn has a reputation as being one of the 'witch-trees' of the countryside, not least because we have to be very careful of its long (and very sharp!) spikes which can puncture skin very easily and the wounds have a tendency to turn septic. The blackthorn is depicted in many fairytales throughout Europe as a tree of ill omen but it along with the alder it is the totem tree of traditional British Old Craft. Called Straif in the Ogham, this tree has the most sinister reputation in Celtic tree lore.

To witches, it often represents the dark side of the Craft since it is a sacred tree to the Dark, or Crone aspect of the Triple

Goddess, and represents the Waning and Dark Moons. Blackthorn is known as the increaser and keeper of dark secrets. The tree is linked with warfare, wounding and death, associated with the Cailleach - the Crone of Death, and the Morrigan. Winter begins when the Cailleach (the Goddess of Winter) strikes the ground with her blackthorn staff. The shrub has a long and often sinister history and is considered the opposite of the benign hawthorn but where blackthorn grows near the white (haw)thorn, the site is especially magical. The blackthorn's spines are extremely hard and can cause a great deal of bleeding, They were frequently used as pins by English witches and became known as the 'pin of slumber'. The shrub was denounced as a witch's tool by the church and therefore the wood of the blackthorn was often used for the pyres of witches and heretics. Remember where those blossoms are and we know where to find the sloes to make our sloe gin ...

Nevertheless, for those who know about these things, the blackthorn is also seen as a protective tree and representative of the endless cycle of life and death. For all its deadly associations the blossoms were used in ancient fertility rites as well as being hung in the bedchamber of a bride on her wedding night. It provides blossom whilst there is still snow on the ground while everything else still seems comatose from its winter sleep; its dense branches protect the year's new chicks from predation and in their adulthood provides them with food when many other species of plant have lost their berries. Witches in northern England would carve the symbol for thorn on a blackthorn staff for protection and the tree itself is also said to be protected by the Faere Folk. It is considered a 'fairy tree' and is protected by the *Lunantishee*, a type of fairy that inhabits it. They will not allow a mortal to cut blackthorn on 11th May or 11th November - the original dates of Beltaine (May Day) and Samhain (All Hallows Eve) according to the Old Calendar. Great misfortune would befall anyone who ignored this advice. [*Folklore and Tradition of the Irish Hedgerow*]

Hawthorn is at its most prominent in the landscape when it blossoms during the month of May, and probably the most popular of its many vernacular names is the May-tree. Traditionally it should blossom at Beltaine and in Old Craft we say it's not Beltaine until the tree is in flower and its sensual perfume wafts across the fields. It is also known as a Faere Tree for it is said to guard the entrance to the faerie realm and it is still considered bad luck to harm one. In the next field we have a 'Faerie Fold' surrounded by hawthorn trees and locals cannot be cajoled or bribed to cut up and take away an oak tree felled by the winter gales on the site.

The hawthorn has many uses, the young leaves are eaten and were commonly referred to as bread and cheese; the blossom and berries were made into wines and jellies, and decoctions of the flowers and leaves were used to stabilise blood pressure. Young leaves and flower buds are used as both a food eaten in spring salads, and as a medicine. Medicinally, an infusion is prepared which has been shown to be valuable in improving the heartbeat rate and strength, especially after heart failure; it also helps with irregular heartbeats and improves the peripheral circulation. The berries are gathered in the autumn and have similar medicinal properties – they can be used fresh or dried in a decoction or infused in brandy to make a heart tonic for the winter months. For culinary use the berries are traditionally gather after the first frost which converts some of the starches to sugar and makes the berries more palatable. Berries are used as an ingredient in hedgerow wine, or to make haw jelly as an accompaniment to wild game. Like the blackthorn (from the same family), sprays of Plum and Damson blossom can be seen in the old orchard along **The Path**, because again the white flowers appear before the leaves. The trees flower in early spring and cover the tree in blossom but if there is a late frost, the tree could lose all of its flowers, and there may not be any fruit at all if the frost is severe enough. Here

Wild Cherry or cultivated trees that have gone feral produce a profusion of white blossom, while Crab Apple and apple blossom surely ranks as one of the loveliest of them all whether we find it in the hedgerow or in the gardens.

These are our first moments of 'me-time' awareness. The soft grey-green of the woodbine against the bare twigs and branches of the hedge is a reminder that in a few months' time the heady fragrance of the wild honeysuckle will assail our senses as we walk past. It was believed that if honeysuckle grew around the entrance to the home it prevented ill luck from entering. In other places it was believed that grown around the doors it will attract good luck. If it grows well in our own garden, then we will be protected from negativity.

In Ireland honeysuckle was believed to have a power against bad spirits, and it was used in a drink to cure the effects of the evil eye; while bringing the flowers into the house will bring money with them. In the Victorian era there was a ban on young girls bringing honeysuckle into the home because the heady fragrance of the flowers was believed to cause dreams that were far too risqué for their sensibilities. Despite its lack of any real economic use, honeysuckle was regarded as a 'lower division of the wood' in some versions of the old Irish Brehon laws on trees and shrubs. It was also linked by some medieval scholars with the ancient Irish Ogham alphabet.

The blossoming of the blackthorn, plum, cherry and apple provide us with that reason to 'stand and stare' echoing the Japanese flower-viewing tradition of *hanami* – the custom of enjoying the transient beauty of flowers. And once we've developed the habit of 'staring' we also begin to sense the history, myths, folklore, superstition and wort-lore connected with these familiar, everyday connections. It may also surprise us to learn that these superstitions and folklore are now recognised as a vital part of the development of the human race, rather than just a confused jumble of traditional children's stories. It is also accepted that at the root of these superstitions is a serious philosophy that was not random and which had its own peculiar logic, even if this is not rationalistic logic that sits comfortable within the remit of modern society. For the practitioner of witchcraft, it is necessary to wade through an irritating maze of analogies, allegories, symbols - all of which means making connections between things which outwardly and rationally are not connected at all.

Myths and legends that might, at first glance, seem merely products of childish fancy are very far from being merely fanciful and are the means by which ancient peoples expressed their fundamental notions of life and Nature. These enduring superstitions and folklore are the actual methods by which our Ancestors expressed certain ways of viewing the 'rules' of life and which were brought into existence by the manner in which life was regulated in their society; the folklore reflecting the morality according to the lights of their time.

Because when we talk about the folklore of a people or culture, we are referring to the whole body of traditional beliefs, customs, and stories of a community, passed through the generations by word of mouth, together with the various attempts that have been made to explain these ancient narratives for the benefit of *modern* thinking. The real function of these stories, however, was to strengthen the existing tradition and endow it with a greater value and prestige by tracing it back to a higher, better, more 'supernatural' reality of ancient times. What men have thought about their folk traditions *is* important not only for what it may tell us about their perspective of life and death as the ancients viewed them, but for what it tells us about humankind today. *If nothing else, it shows what we have lost!*

The rational folklore and myths were those that represented the gods as beautiful and wise; but the *real* difficulties presented by mythology spring from its irrational elements, which to modern minds can appear unnatural, senseless or even repellent. It is to these *irrational* elements that the witch must turn if they wish to reconnect with the Old Ways, which still lie at the very heart of traditional witchcraft. For the true seeker, those great tales and legends remain 'true' stories; not because we think they really happened but because they contain certain 'universal truths' about humanity and life; truths which cannot be translated into plain statement. And we must 'believe' in them in the same way as our Ancestors did in order to make that vital spiritual link between the then and now.

And much of these Old Ways are waiting to be discovered via a rekindling of interest in our local flora and fauna. Along *The Path* of the urban wood and field margin there are all manner of different trees – mostly oak and birch – but away from the daily tramp of dog walkers and strollers we can get a glimpse of the dark shadow of the dense, ancient holly wood from where this SSSI (site of special scientific interest) takes its name, because it is a protected area. Under Brehon Law, the old Gaelic legal system, holly was among the protected trees. Moving to medieval times, it was classified among the most precious species of trees, also including oak, hazel, yew, ash, pine and apple, which were called 'nobles of the wood'.

In Celtic mythology the Holly King was said to rule over the half of the year from the Summer to the Winter Solstice, at which time the Oak King defeated the Holly King to rule for the time until the Summer Solstice came around again. These two aspects of the Nature god were later incorporated into mummers' plays traditionally performed around Yuletide. The Holly King was depicted as a powerful giant of a man covered in holly leaves and branches, and wielding a holly bush as a club and may well have been the archetype on which the Green Knight of Arthurian legend was based.

However, the folklore of the holly is not solely connected with Yuletide festivities. In European folklore, holly trees were believed to offer protection from lightning strikes and were planted near houses for that reason. Like several other native trees, it was felt to have protective properties, and there were taboos against cutting down a whole tree. Hollies were frequently left uncut in hedges when these were trimmed. A more arcane reason for this was to obstruct witches who were known to run along the tops of hedges, though more practically farmers used their distinctive evergreen shapes to establish lines of sight during winter ploughing! And all these things will flit through our minds as we stroll along the foot-worn trails of urban wood.

Tucked away in the bottom of the hedgerow we keep an eye open for the Common Dog Violet, a familiar little wildflower of woodland, heath, old pasture and grassy hedge-banks this blue-violet flower is always solitary on the stem The dark-green, heart-shaped leaves are on long, slender stalks. It flowers from April to June, but its blooms are not scented, unlike those of its cousin, the Sweet Violet, which was used as a perfume in Ancient Greece. Gerard's *Herbal* suggests that 'The flowers are good for all inflammations, especially of the sides and lungs. They take away hoarseness of the chest, the ruggedness of the windpipe and jaws and take away thirst', while Culpeper says that 'they ease pains in the head, caused through want of sleep.' Shakespeare was a great fan of the violet and references to it appear in at least eighteen passages of his works but then his hometown of Stratford-upon-Avon was renowned for its magnificent displays of violets in early spring.

Another spring-time favourite found in the woods is the Primrose. The symbol of safety and protection, in ancient times it was placed on the doorstep to encourage the Faere Folk to bless the house and anyone living in it. It was the flower of love and bringer of good luck, and was the symbol of the first day of spring - and as such was laid across thresholds to welcome 'May Day'. Also considered to be a bringer of great inspiration for poets, it is a flower of youth, birth, sweetness and tenderness. The primrose was said to be highly-prized by the Druids and its abundance in woods and pastures made it an easily-collectible plant.

The primrose has many medicinal uses and was important in the past as a remedy for muscular rheumatism, paralysis and gout. The leaves and flowers were used either fresh or dried; the roots being dried before use. Culpepper was aware of the healing properties of the primrose and said, 'Of the leaves of Primrose is made as fine a salve to heal wounds as any I know'. In the Middle Ages an infusion of the roots was used to treat headaches. In Irish folklore it was believed that rubbing a toothache with a primrose leaf for two minutes would relieve the pain.

Often dismissed as a weed, the invasive but attractive Herb Robert was believed to be the plant of a house-goblin in England, Robin Goodfellow. Geoffrey Grigson, in his classic compendium of British plant lore, *The Englishman's Flora*, notes the ancient familiarity of this common dooryard weed, and the uncommon degree of attention it seems to have commanded over the centuries, as is evidenced by the more than one hundred local names attested for it in England alone. Many names include the name Robert or its diminutive, Robin; some link the plant to the Ronin, often viewed as a dangerous bird in European folklore, which could bring illness, death, or bad luck into the house.

Whatever sinister associations it may have acquired in European folklore, Herb Robert was a valued medicinal plant in the Middle Ages. In chapter CXLIV of the *Physica*, Hildegard of Bingen remarks on the very hot nature of 'cranschnabel', whose power she compares to that of exotic spices. Hildegard recommends a powder made of Herb Robert mixed with a little powdered feverfew or nutmeg sprinkled and eaten on bread, or licked from the hand, for pain in the heart. The medieval herbalist's *Herba Sancti Ruperti*, it has five cranes-bill type petals with rounded ends, five-lobed leaves and thin, reddish, stems. The latter are often quite hairy and produce a strong, unpleasant smell. For all that it is difficult to eradicate, the overall appearance of the plant is one of fragility.

Perhaps one of our most familiar flowers of all, the Common Daisy can be seen flowering almost all year-round. Its persistent and widespread growth, heralding the arrival of spring to our gardens, has resulted in children using its flowers to make daisy chains, and adults desperately trying to rid their lawns of this so-called 'weed'. The flowers open up to greet the morning sun, and are visited throughout the day by an eclectic assortment of insects before closing up again as the light fades. Instead of investing the considerable energy and time it takes to rid the garden of daisies, a lot of people choose to live with this cheerful little flower. It's a decision that does no real harm, since it adds a certain charm and can be a great boon to the wildlife that increasingly rely on our urban gardens.

Daisies are also widely recognised as a healing herb. The plant used to have a great reputation for treating fresh wounds, and a distillation from the plant was once taken as a treatment for inflammatory disorders of the liver. In the 14th century the daisy was the principal ingredient in an ointment widely used to treat wounds, gout and fevers. Daisies have often been championed in literature, and Chaucer described them as his favourite flower, the 'day's eye' and the only plant that could 'soften all my sorrows', while Shelley likened the flowers of the daisy to earthbound stars.

Wherever we walk along *The Path* we cannot avoid that plague of garden, meadows and waste ground – the Dandelion, that vibrant harbinger of spring. But for all its long medicinal and folk-history, perhaps the flower's most important use is helping the survival of endangered bumblebees and wild solitary bees who are going hungry because of a lack of food in the landscape – and dandelions are 'super food' for hungry bees. By allowing dandelions to bloom we are helping wild bees to pollinate fruit crops and plants and to halt the decline of certain bee species that are in danger of disappearing altogether.

Nettles are also a magnet for wildlife and can be a surprisingly versatile ingredient in the kitchen. The nettle we're used to in the UK is Urtica dioica, a perennial plant full of iron, calcium, magnesium and nitrogen, which makes it incredibly nutritious. For a hearty nettle soup, you'll need about 200g of fresh nettle tips; add 450g of potatoes, peeled and cubed, a dash of cream and one litre of stock. Boil the potatoes until soft and steam the nettles. Drain the spuds and add the nettles and stock. Bring the boil, whisk with a hand blender, add the dash of cream and season. Nettles can also be used in exactly the same way as spinach – almost any recipe containing spinach could contain young nettles as an alternative. For a simple side dish, they're best steamed for around five minutes. But don't use after July or they become a laxative!

Along the barren verges bright yellow Coltsfoot makes its presence felt. This was a plant awaited with genuine concern by country people of old, for it was from this plant that a remedy was compounded for long-lasting winter coughs; it was a favourite herb with ancient apothecaries who often use it for infections of the lungs. Coltsfoot is a perennial plant that looks similar to a dandelion when it blooms in spring. This wild edible plant is unusual in that the flowers bloom and die before the appearance of any leaves; it is one of the first plants to flower in late winter, heralding the beginning of spring.

Believed to call the fairies when rung, and thought to be unlucky to walk through, a mass of Bluebells was said to be full of spells. It is also considered an unlucky flower to pick or bring into the house. Not all of the bluebell's folklore is quite so gloomy - by wearing a wreath made of the flowers, the wearer would be compelled to speak only truth. Where bluebells are found in hedgerows may indicate an old wood, as their presence is indicative of ancient woodland.

In the woods the floor is swept clear for the entrance of the ballet of the bluebells, a sheer delight and a tree-to-tree carpet of colour, providing harvest of nectar for the bees as well as a feast for the human eye. The misty blue avenues between the columns of a beech wood conjure up vision of a cathedral, and in the imagination of the onlooker it needs only the sound of an organ playing Bach's *Toccata and Fugue* to complete the effect. Such is the magic of bluebells. [*The Country Book of the Year*]

Perhaps it *is* easier to become aware of trees and plants in winter and spring. An oak is an oak, but an oak tree on **The Path** is just a little bit different from all the other trees. And after a while, we'll be able to distinguish it from its fellows. The following example is a variation on the theme of the 'mystical mug' when it comes to looking at trees. Here we imagine we are standing in front of an apple tree in the old orchard in autumn, and on the side facing us are lots of red apples. We automatically assume that the other side of the tree will also be laden with red apples. When we walk around the tree to take a look, however, we notice that the apples are more yellow than we'd expected. Because that side of the tree has had less sun ...

Similarly, pussy-willow catkins and hazel's yellow 'lamb's tails' dust pollen on the wind and are easily recognized in the spring. Most of the objects that we see are three-dimensional, and we cannot encompass them with just one look. If we want to become aware of the tree in its natural habitat, we have to look at it from different angles. We have to make several observations of the individual trees, observing it from different angles and at varying times of the year, all of which adds perspective to our view of each particular tree. Spring offers us the opportunity to catch-up with old friends as all life – the whole glorious parade along **The Path** - dresses up in its Eostre finery.

Exercise: A Sense of Awareness

Do not obsess about finding absolute silence because you will never find it. Just find a space away from the hustle and bustle of everyday life. There will still be sounds: cars passing, dogs barking, clocks ticking, birds singing, your stomach gurgling. Just ignore the sounds, let them pass and allow your mind to settle.

Awareness – or 'mindfulness' to give it its more popular tag - is the state of being conscious, or the quality of being 'perceptually knowledgeable'. It is also the ability to perceive, feel, know, or be cognizant of events. Mindfulness is about finding some space in the mind, less judgemental, a with greater sense of perspective, in which we see this fundamental truth for ourselves in a very direct and personal way.

> It is about recognizing that just because a thought appears in the mind, we are not that thought, and just because we might feel a certain way at a particular time, we are not that feeling. It is the difference between being in a storm and witnessing a storm. It is the difference between being outside in that storm, swept away by the wind and the rain, and sitting inside, cozy and warm by the fire, as you watch the storm pass by. [*Psychology Today*]

Today, there are many superficial approaches to meditation but five minutes with Nature can often be more beneficial than a whole programme of meditative exercises and yoga classes. Try this simple approach …

> Find a wild place where you can sit quiet and undisturbed for an hour. If it has the sound of (and sight of) water so much the better. Open yourself to the four elements – earth, water, air and fire. Earth is the ground beneath you and the whole planet; water is beside you and also makes up 70% of your

body; air is all around you enabling you to live and breathe; the fire of the sun enables the Mother to come to life, and the sun is always there even behind clouds and in the dark of the night.

Be still there, watch and hear the water, allow it to run through your body, feelings and mind, washing away the Winter of the past and leaving you fresh and clean for the coming newness of Spring. When the water has cleansed you, you'll feel the process turn itself off, and you feel yourself return to the everyday world ... but different, with a new perspective on your life. Thank the water, and the goddess, and the god, for what they have given you. The water may ask for a gift in return, this can be as simple as to promise to listen more and notice both nature and otherworld around you all the time. Give your gift and say you will return to visit with them again.

This piece is reproduced with the kind permission of esoteric author Elen Sentier from her Spring newsletter.

The Wild Larder

We have lost so much of the knowledge that our forebears took for granted. For instance, there are many plant leaves that can be collected and added to salads or cooked as a vegetable ...

... such as Chickweed and those without gardens should be able to find some by any waste ground or field edge even in the winter months. The leaves are oval, bright green and soft and can be picked in almost any month of the year except when there has been a hard frost; it also flowers throughout the year, with tiny white, star-like blossoms. Chickweed is one of the tenderest of wild greens, with a taste resembling corn salad or a mild lettuce. Pick in bunches, including the stems, wash and put into a saucepan without any additional water. Add a knob of butter and some chopped spring onions; simmer gently for no more than two minutes and serve with a dash of lemon juice.

... and Jack-by-the-hedge that is perfect for those who like garlic but only in moderation and which can be picked as early as February if there's been a mild winter. The plant grows on waysides, hedge banks and open woodland and can be easily identified by gently bruising the leaves to release a faint garlic smell. The leaves, finely chopped can be added to salads or in a sauce for lamb, mixed with hawthorn buds and a little garden mint, vinegar and sugar.

Start simple and begin to use these wild plants in your kitchen.

Chapter Three

Summer - the Path of Flowers

Since prehistory, the Summer Solstice has been seen as a significant time of year in many cultures, and has been marked by diverse festivals and rituals. According to the astronomical definition of the seasons, the summer solstice also marks the beginning of summer, which lasts until the Autumnal Equinox (22nd or 23rd September in the Northern Hemisphere, or 20th or 21st March in the Southern Hemisphere). Traditionally, the Summer Solstice is seen as the *middle* of summer and referred to as 'Midsummer'. Within the Arctic Circle (for the northern hemisphere) or Antarctic Circle (for the southern hemisphere), there is continuous daylight around the Summer Solstice.

The woods of *The Path* with its scattering of fading bluebells, horsetails and ferns, have a primeval feel about them as spring descends into summer; and when the trees are full of leaf, it is easy to image that we are tramping through Wildwood even though we are never more than a few hundred yards from our village or town. The urban woods along *The Path* are somewhat unkempt and before the wooded path opens out into the meadow there is a sturdy oak which is exposed to the full force of the westerly winds. The branches on the windward side break the gusts: the trunk and the dark, sturdier branches don't give an inch, the smaller branches and twigs sway but a little. Then a branch breaks off ... Next to the oak is a silver birch that sways and bends with the force of the summer storm ...

Later, we recall the buffeting of the wind and feel so much empathy for the two trees that we can almost experience or perceive what forces were at play. We can feel the resistance and stiffness of the oak, and how futile this resistance is when a branch gets broken off. With the birch, we can feel how it surrenders itself to the wind and how supple and pliable the tree is. We can attribute resistance to an oak and pliability to a birch and if these concepts are correct, then we will be able to recognise them in all the different parts of these trees. We will see it in the leaves (the tough, unbending leaves of the oak and the light rustling leaves of the birch) and the seeds (the heavy acorn with the hard shell, the light birch seeds which carry on the wind) ... [*Psychology Today*]

It is the Ash tree, however, that has a host of folklore surrounding it. The ash along with the oak is one of the last trees to come into leaf and according to country lore, the one that comes into leaf first, gives us an indication as to what the weather will be like for the summer: "Ash before the Oak, you can expect a soak, but Oak before the Ash, expect a little splash" The fascination of the ash tree traces its roots to the ancient times. The Druids believed that it had the ability to direct and blend the masculine and feminine energy, using a branch of the ash to make their staffs. The staff then acted as a connection between the realms of the earth and the sky. A staff of ash is hung over door frames for protection as it will ward off evil influences; while ash leaves can be scattered in the four directions to protect the house against negative and psychic attacks - but despite its role in protecting against witches, the ash is also extensively used *by* them.

The ash is often found growing near sacred wells and it has been suggested that there is a connection between the tree and the healing waters of the well (possibly iron contained in the roots and leeching into the well). The tree itself can sometimes supply 'holy' water as the bole of the ash often has a hollow in it like a shallow bowl; the water that gathers in this is well known for its healing properties. This could be a good example of a Bile - a sacred tree. Sailors also believed that if they carved a piece of ash wood into the shape of a solar cross and carried it with them then they would be protected from drowning. A solar cross, consisting of an equilateral cross inside a circle ⊕ is frequently found in the symbolism of prehistoric cultures, particularly during the Neolithic to Bronze Age periods of European prehistory.

The oak, birch and ash are common tree along *The Path* and we should make an effort to recognize and understand the life-cycle of these three sacred trees that are tightly bound into our folk-, country- and Craft-lore.

As we leave the woods and step onto *The Path* that borders the meadow our attention is caught by the plants that adorn the verge of hard-packed earth and stones: daisies, dandelions and filmy cow parsley. Cow parsley (*Anthriscus sylvestris*), grows in sunny to semi-shaded locations in meadows and at the edges of hedgerows and woodland. It is related to other diverse members of the Apiaceae family, such as parsley, carrot, hemlock and hogweed - and often confused with *Daucus carota* which is known as Queen Anne's lace or wild carrot and mistaken for several similar-looking poisonous plants, among them poison hemlock and fool's parsley.

From where *The Path* exits the woods it is only a few minutes before we come to the plank bridge over a brook fringed with forget-me-nots. The plank bridge is one of our favourite places to dawdle with the pond on one side and the brook making its way back into the woods on the other. On one side the water lies dark and deep in a languid pool where dragonflies and nymphs hover over the still surface (perfect for scrying); and from this bridge the slope of the water meadow basks in late summer sunlight and autumn mists since the surrounding ancient woodland was cut back for agricultural reasons. 'It is widely acknowledged that a landscape of open fields, trees and brooks is what humans consider most beautiful,' observes Chet Raymo.

In the water meadow we can find an olde English favourite:

Meadowsweet from the Anglo-Saxon meodu-swete meaning 'Mead sweetener'. The plant's herbal uses had a base in scientific fact; in common with many other folk and herbal remedies, in the 19th century, chemists isolated salicylic acid from meadowsweet to use as a disinfectant that not only made rooms smell better but helped the fight against bacteria. It was one of the three herbs considered sacred by the Druids: the others being vervain and water mint.

Creamy, perennial of damp waysides, meadows, marshes and woods, this tall plant flowers from June to September, and with a heavy fragrance, the flower heads are frequently visited by bees attracted by the heavy scent which can be so evocative of summer days in the countryside. In spite of this fragrance, however, the flowers produce no nectar. Insects, however, don't realise this but their visits serve to fertilise the plants which are heavy with pollen. A peculiarity of this flower is that the scent of the leaves is quite different from that of the flowers, the leaves having a heavy almond-like aroma whereas the flowers have a strong sweet smell.

Meadowsweet was historically known as Bridewort because it was strewn on the ground at hand-fastings for the bride to walk on (*wort* is an old word that means herb or root) and it was also used in wedding posies and bridal bouquets. Meadowsweet was also spread on the floor in medieval times to provide a nice smell and deter insects. This plant was given to Cúchulainn in liquid form and it was said to calm his fits of rage and outbreaks of fever and it may be for this reason that another name for meadowsweet in Ireland is Cuchulainn's Belt or Crios Conchulainn. It is also associated with death as the scent of its flowers was said to induce a sleep that was deep and fatal. However, in County Galway it was believed that if a person was wasting away because of faerie influence then putting some meadowsweet under the bed ensured that they would be cured by the morning.

All along the water courses most Willow species grow and thrive and this theme is reflected in the legends and magic associated with these trees. The willow muse, called Heliconian (after Helike), was sacred to poets, and the Greek poet Orpheus carried willow branches on his adventures in the Underworld. He was also given a lyre by Apollo, and it is interesting to note that the sound boxes of harps used to be carved from solid willow wood. The willow is also associated with the *fey* and the *'Wind in the Willows'* is said to be the whisperings of a faerie in the ear of a poet.

Willow was often the tree most sought by village wise-women, since it has so many medicinal properties, and eventually its healing and religious qualities became one and the tree became called a 'witch's tree'. The willow is associated with enchantment, wishing, romantic love, healing, protection, fertility, death, femininity, divination friendship, joy, love, and peace. Placed in homes, willow branches protect against evil and malign sorcery. Carried, the wood bestows bravery, dexterity, and helps to overcome the fear of death. If we knock on a willow tree ('knock on wood') this will avert evil. A willow growing near a home will protect it from danger, while they are also good trees to plant around cemeteries and for lining graves because of its symbolism of death and protection.

Willow can also be used in rituals for intuition, knowledge, gentle nurturing, and will elucidate the feminine qualities of both men and women. When a person needs to get something off their chest or to share a secret, if they confess to a Willow, their secret will be trapped. Also, wishes are granted by a willow if they are asked for in the correct manner. Willow leaves, bark and wood add energy to healing magic, and burning a mix of willow bark and sandalwood during the waning moon can help to conjure spirits. Uses of willow in love talismans include using the leaves to attract love.

The tree is linked to grief and in the 16th and 17th centuries jilted lovers would wear wreaths of willow and many unrequited love poems were written that included reference to the tree. In Irish folklore it couldn't be more different as it was called sail ghlann grin or the 'bright cheerful sallow'. There it was considered lucky to take a sally-rod with you on a journey and sally withies were placed around a milk churn to ensure good butter. It was believed that the charcoal left behind after burning willow could be crushed and spread on the back of an animal as a way of increasing fertility and even restoring hair.

Needless to say, country folk have long been familiar with the healing properties of willow. They made an infusion from the bitter bark as a remedy for colds and fevers, and to treat inflammatory conditions such as rheumatism. Young willow twigs were also chewed to relieve pain. In the early 19th century modern science isolated the active ingredient responsible, salicylic acid, which was also found in the meadowsweet plant.

As we follow the brook back through the wood along a different pathway, in the sunlit glades swathes of foxgloves stand tall above the bracken. A well-loved plant, the whole foxglove plant is extremely poisonous, but provides a source of digitalis used by doctors in heart medicine. The foxglove was believed to keep evil at bay if grown in the garden, but it was considered unlucky to bring the blooms inside the house. The name derives from the shape of the flowers resembling the fingers of a glove – 'folk's glove' meaning belonging to the Faere Folk and folklore tells that bad faerie gave the flowers to the fox to put on his feet to soften his steps whilst hunting. In Irish folklore it was said that if a child was wasting away then it was under the influence of the faerie (fairy stroke) and foxglove was given to counteract this as it was known to revive people. One such remedy was the juice of twelve leaves taken daily. It could also work for adults, such a person would be given a drink made from the leaves, if they were not too far gone, they would drink it and get sick but then recover. However, if they were completely under the spell of the faerie then they would refuse to drink. An amulet of foxglove could also cure the urge to keep travelling that resulted when anyone stepped onto the faerie grass, the 'stray sod' or *fód seachrán*. In Ireland it is also believed that the foxglove will nod its head if one of the 'gentry' pass by.

And it's not just in the woods and fields that Nature is lush and tropical and green, because as *The Path* takes us passed the allotments, we can find the lushness reflected in the vegetable plots and gardens. In the overgrown orchard some of the old trees are still capable of producing a good crop after the warm, damp start to the year. With our newly discovered vision we relish the sight of all this bounty that is the result of sore backs and chapped hands during the cold and wet of the seedtime. As harvest approaches, we can appreciate the fruit of their labours by proxy since friendly gardeners often have surplus stocks that they gladly share with their neighbours.

Exercise: A Sense of Contemplation

Don't get carried away by a new-found enthusiasm but commit to contemplate *today* – and *only today*. It is not necessary to commit to contemplation tomorrow, or every day for a week, a month, a year because over-commitment is a sure-fire recipe for procrastination. If you have the opportunity for five minutes contemplation today – contemplate today. If you have the opportunity to contemplate tomorrow – contemplate tomorrow.

Contemplation is the action of looking thoughtfully at something for a long time. It is not a relaxation exercise or meditation but while it may contribute to us becoming more relaxed, this is simply a side effect. Contemplation is profound thinking about something and here we select something from the natural world where we can sit and stare at – for example - bees on a clover patch, lavender plant or butterfly bush (buddleia).

Doctorates in Bioenergetic Medicine and teachers of the ancient Egyptian healing and spiritual tradition, Meredith

McCord and Jill Schumacher tell us that in ancient Egypt the humming sound of the bee was said to stimulate the release of super hormones known as the 'Elixirs of Metamorphosis', as the sound also resonates the ventricular chambers in the center of the brain, which are filled with cerebrospinal fluid that acts as a cushion for the brain's cortex, providing basic mechanical and immunological protection to the brain inside the skull. The good doctors claim that the humming sounds of bees also resonate and stimulate various other structures of the brain, including the pineal gland, pituitary gland, the hypothalamus that link the nervous system to the endocrine system, and amygdala, which is responsible for emotions, survival instincts, and memory.

Five minutes contemplation in the company of these small creatures can open up worlds that we would otherwise not bother to think about – and it's an added incentive to create areas in our garden that are bee-friendly for our own benefit, too. Invest is a couple of bee boxes to encourage queen bees to lay eggs and repopulate your own garden next spring.

The Wild Larder

We can also treasure the time spent alone foraging. The repetition of gathering wild food allows the mind to relax – we can't fret about household chores and work when we're out there stocking up our wild larder.

The creamy-white flowers of the Elder can be found in woods, hedgerows and waste places and as Richard Mabey writes in *Food For Free*:

...to see the mangy, decaying skeletons of elders in the winter, we would not think the tree was any use to man or beast. Nor would the acrid stench of the young leaves in spring change your opinion. But by the end of June the whole shrub is covered with great sprays of sweet-smelling flowers, for which there are probably more uses than any other single species of blossom...

Elderflowers can be eaten fresh from the shrub on a hot summer's day and have the taste of a frothy ice-cream soda; while the flowers separated from the stalks make a remarkable sparkling wine. Dipped in batter the flower-heads can be deep-fried and served as fritters to end a summer meal. The berries are small and green at first, ripening to deep purple clusters that weigh down the branches. These are made into wine, chutney, jellies and ketchup.

Any witch worth her salt, of course, knows that the elder is also known as the 'poor man's medicine chest' due to the wide range of herbal remedies that can be got from the shrub. The flowers are utilised to raise the resistance to respiratory infections, and ointment made from elder flowers is excellent for chilblains and stimulating localised circulation. The flowers are also used in hay fever treatments for their anti-catarrhal properties. Medicinally, both the berries and the flowers encourage fever response and stimulates sweating, which prevents very high temperatures and provides an important channel for detoxification. To cure warts, rub them with a green elder twig which should then be buried. As the wood rots so the wart will disappear.

Chapter Four

Autumn – the Path of Harvest

The Autumnal Equinox occurs the moment the sun crosses the celestial equator – the imaginary line in the sky above Earth's equator – from north to south. This happens either on 22nd, 23rd, or 24th September every year. According to the astronomical definition of the seasons, the Autumnal Equinox also marks the beginning of autumn, which lasts until the Winter Solstice ... Seasons are opposite on either side of the Equator, so the equinox in September is also known as the Autumnal (or fall) Equinox in the Northern Hemisphere, and is considered the first day of autumn. In the Southern Hemisphere, it is known as the Vernal (spring) Equinox and marks the first day of spring.

As leaves begin to fall, through a clearing in the trees we get a glimpse of the rugged granite outcrop that overlooks this patch of urban woodland. These rocks are of volcanic origin and are very old, dating back through 600 million years to Precambrian times, formed from molten lava deep within the sedimentary rocks, cooling slowly to produce hard, blocky rock with large crystals. To reach the outcrop we need to follow *The Path* through the woods, along the field margin and over the old stone canal bridge to the gap in the hedge that leads to the summit. But that is a walk for another day...

At this time of Keat's 'mists and mellow fruitfulness' we need to look at our familiar walk through a different pair of eyes. If, for example, a biologist, a forester, an artist and an architect were walking through the same woodland they would probably all be seeing something different. The biologist would see the varied species of tree and perhaps note all sorts of peculiarities. The forester would identify the different species as well as the shape of the trunk, and be able to estimate the volume of wood available for cutting. The artist would see the many shades of green, brown and grey, while the architect's attention might be drawn to the relationship between length and thickness of the trunk, and the span of the canopy.

In other words, they would all looking at the same thing, but seeing it from a different perspective, a different interest and a different set of concepts. When they go home, they will all have a different story to tell about their visit to the wood. The biologist will remember the number of different species; the forester will talk about the quality of the wood ready for cutting and what the yield will be. The artist and the architect, on the other hand, might not even be able to answer the question as to what kind of trees grew in the wood, but the shape and density of the trees will have had a profound effect of their minds. Everyone's observations will be different because they are the result of *personal* interest and a personally developed set of concepts. As a consequence, everyone perceives their environment differently.

A pagan perspective, however, should encompass *all* of these varied concepts and they should see the types of tree growing there according to country-lore and the bounty yielded from a tree's individual uses; they will empathise with the beauty and spirituality of the wood, coupled with the forms that please the aesthetic senses. For the seasons are changing and already the leaves have turned to gold on the silver birch and there is a nip in the air where the early morning mist is slow to clear. The cathedral-quiet of the autumn wood envelopes us in its silence.

September makes its sweeping entry and the scene is set with the brilliant colour of gold and the rich smell of fruit cake, the promise of the autumn. The fruits of a million plants glitter in the hedgerows like so many jewels in a crown. In the morning the cool air greets the sun, a tandem of dewdrops sparkle from every spider's web. [*The Country Book of the Year*]

The early morning dog-walk takes on a whole new perspective as we walk along *The Path* towards the allotments where there are plenty of late-summer vegetables waiting to be harvested. There is a strange tranquility about this time of the year as we fast approach the Autumnal Equinox. As we cross the plank bridge, we watch one or two swallows skim across the surface, picking up the final hatches of fly before joining their fellows on the overhead wires. They are eager to be off, leaving an empty gap in our lives as the chill of autumn draws near.

It's often during the autumn and winter months that we become aware of the sheer number of different species of wildlife that inhabit our towns and village butting up to these urban woodlands and SSSI sites. At first thought our gardens would appear to be inhospitable to wildlife, and while the timider creatures shun urban areas, many others thrive in the 'concrete jungle', which offers a surprisingly large number of green places and diverse habitats. Many plants and animals have found a completely new niche for themselves in our urban environment, and some species are now almost completely dependent on town and city life for survival.

Of all the habitats within easy reach of *The Path*, none is more frequented and yet more likely to be overlooked as a haven for wildlife than the suburban garden, which can so quickly become colonized by the flora and fauna from the countryside nearby. Where these two habitats meet -the border zone between concrete and green – it becomes especially rich in wildlife. And as autumn approaches, we can encourage these creatures to visit by offering food and water as their natural supplies diminish. Peek into your neighbours' gardens and see what ideas you can adopt for your own.

Because all along *The Path* and often in gardens, the title of 'queen of autumn' must surely go to the Rowan, or mountain ash, with its profusion of bright scarlet berries. In early Irish law the tree was classified as Aithig fedo or 'Commoner of The Wood' and its mythic roots go back to classical times. Greek mythology tells of how Hebe, the goddess of youth, dispensed rejuvenating ambrosia to the gods from her magical chalice. When, through carelessness, she lost this cup to demons, the gods sent an eagle to recover the cup. The feathers and drops of blood which the eagle shed in the ensuing fight with the demons fell to earth, where each of them turned into a rowan tree. Hence the tree derived the shape of its leaves from the eagle's feathers and the appearance of its berries from the droplets of blood.

In Ireland the rowan has a long and popular history in folklore as a tree which protects against witchcraft and enchantment. The physical characteristics of the tree may have contributed to its protective reputation, since the tiny five-pointed star or pentagram on each berry opposite its stalk and the pentagram being an ancient protective symbol. The colour red was deemed to be the best protection against enchantment, and so the rowan's vibrant display of berries in autumn may have further contributed to its protective abilities, as suggested in the old rhyme: *'Rowan tree and red thread make the witches tine* [meaning 'to lose'] *their speed'.*

There are several recurring themes of protection offered by the rowan. The tree itself was said to afford protection to the dwelling by which it grew, and pieces of rowan would be hung in the house to protect it from fire. It was also used to keep the dead from rising and tied to a hound's collar to increase its speed. Sprigs of rowan were used as a protection for cattle and against supernatural forces that may threaten the dairy products. It was kept in the byre to safeguard the animals and put in the pail and around the churn to ensure the 'profit' in the milk was not stolen. We also find records of instances as late as the latter half of the 20th-century of people being warned against removing or damaging a rowan in the garden of their newly purchased home. It was traditionally planted in churchyards since it was considered a protection against evil.

Rowans are also a species that are at home in some of the more challenging parts of our ecosystem such as barren mountainsides. They are also one of the species that bear their male and female flowers on separate trees so that it is necessary to have both genders present in a population in order to produce viable seed. The flowers appear before the leaves in the spring, heralding the start of that season. The fresh flowers and the dried fruits are both used medicinally; they are a diuretic and depurative (or blood purifier), useful as a spring cleansing tonic and for skin conditions such as acne. The bark is used as an astringent and to treat fever and is also gathered in the spring. The leaves are also astringent and diuretic. The unripe fruit is used to treat acne. There is mention of combining the leaves, bark, fruits and flowers together for certain traditional cures; presumably some of these would be in dried form. The ripe fruit is traditionally gathered after the first frost, which sweetens the taste. They are used to prepare sloe gin, or as a winter fruit to add to pies and jams or to brew wine.

The leaves and berries of the rowan are sometimes added to incense to aid divination and to increase psychic powers. It's also believed the bark and berries carried on a person will also aid recuperation, and are added to health and healing sachets, as well as power, luck and success charms. Rowan wood has also been traditionally used for making magic staffs, and its branches used for dowsing or divining. Some believe magic wands made from Rowan are especially effective in ritual when psychic intuition is required.

At first sight a Bramble (or blackberry) thicket looks like an entanglement of barbed wire – and just as pain-inflicting if we get caught up in its thorny tentacles. Brambles are often the dominant lower layer in woods of ancient lineage and they quickly invade modern plantations and roadsides. Once the bramble has cast its shadow over the woodland floor, few other plants can co-exist with it except for bracken, whose fiddleheads can easily snake upwards through the bramble's cat's-cradle of arching shoots.

Despite its prickly thorns, its widespread value to country people as a medicinal herb, a source of refreshing tea and above all as a generous bearer of fruit, dates back to prehistoric times. The fruit is a favourite made into jam or jelly, or used in a variety of pies and tarts. In bygone days, the bramble – in common with many other thorny shrubs and trees – was also believed to be an auspicious plant, a powerful talisman against evil forces. In Ireland if you found a piece of bramble attached to a cow's tail at Beltaine it was considered suspicious as it meant someone was trying to put a spell on the milk. An arch of bramble which had rooted at both ends was believed to have special powers and if you wished to invoke evil spirits you could do so by crawling through the arch at Samhain while making your wish. A bramble arch could also be used to cure. For example, a child with whooping cough could be cured by passing it under the arch three times before breakfast for nine consecutive days while saying 'in bramble, out cough, here I leave the whooping cough'. Medical uses include using the leaves in a cure for diarrhoea in both cattle and people; it could cure dropsy and was considered to have fantastic curative powers for coughs and colds. It was also used for a variety of skin complaints such as scalds, burns, boils, shingles and spots.

In Ireland the flower of the blackberry was a symbol of beauty to the Gaelic poets, and a well-known love ballad has the name *Bláth na Sméar*, or 'Flower of the Blackberry'. Bramble was classed as one of the bushes of the wood in the Old Irish Brehon Laws on trees and shrubs, and there was a fine for cutting it. The root of the bramble was used to make the core for hurling balls and for pipes; and the long shoots were used for wickerwork and even for securing thatch. Blackberries were traditionally eaten mashed up with oatmeal to make a tasty porridge, and for making jam, while the roots were used to make an orange dye.

With the onset of heavy dews and the first frosts, mildew begins to cloud the late berries. In medieval times in England it was a sign that the devil had defiled the crop and it was therefore deemed unwise to pick blackberries after Michaelmas Day (29th September). A similar Irish belief was that the berries were not to be eaten after Samhain because the Púca (one of the faere folk) spits on them and they become inedible (in some parts of Ireland they believe that the Púca urinate on them). So, no more blackberry picking for this year!

In the autumn world by the plank bridge much of the frantic activity of the spring and summer has given way to cooler days. Beds of common reeds can vary in size from narrow waterside fringes to large clumps of drying vegetation; a stand of bulrush come into flower with soft, velvety seed heads that are greatly prized for floral arrangements. The wind in the reeds creates a whispering sound that can be quite eerie as we stand on the bridge and gaze into the dark water below. The pond's surface is littered with brightly coloured leaves that are caught by the current and gently funneled towards the outflow that feeds the brook.

The adjoining allotments and orchard have been harvested and the ground is being prepared for the winter. A time of chilly mornings with the kind of weather that puts us in mind of hot mugs of tea, bowls of soup and if we're an allotment gardener, lots of winter digging! If, on the other hand, we've cast envious looks at all those delicious fresh vegetables but haven't the time or inclination for an allotment, why not spend the next few months investigating the possibility of 'container gardening'. There is no better way of getting closer to Nature than growing (and eating) your own – even if it's only a few popular herbs and home-grown tomatoes to begin with.

Exercise: A Sense of Reflection

Nature tops the list of potent tranquilisers and stress reducers.

The mere sound of running water has been shown to lower blood pressure. When we spend time in Nature, our intuition comes alive and it evokes a feeling hard to put into words. In Japanese they do have a word for it: yugen – which gives a profound sense of the beauty and mystery of the Universe.

If we're talking about well-being and awareness there are two Japanese festivals that are worth incorporating into our lives. Reflecting on colourful autumn foliage is a seasonal event that we can easily adopt since it allows us to connect to the seasons through Nature. Just as the blooming of cherry blossoms is celebrated during *hanami* season in March and April, so are the autumn colours enjoyed before the onset of winter. Searching for the most striking shades of leaf is known as *Momigari* (red leaf hunting) It has been popular in Japan for centuries and for Buddhists, it's a moment which is important both spiritually and symbolically as it reminds us that life is ephemeral.

Tsukimi are the Japanese festivals honoring the autumn moon, a variant of the mid-Autumn Festival. The celebration of the full moon typically takes place on the 15th day of the eighth month of the traditional Japanese calendar; the waxing moon is celebrated on the 13th day of the ninth month. These days normally fall in September and October of the modern solar calendar. The tradition dates to the Heian era, and is now so popular in Japan that some people repeat the activities for several evenings following the appearance of the full moon during the eighth luni-solar month.

At these times, we literally just 'stand and stare' at the natural spectacle taking place before our eyes – as we take in the beauty and wonder of the brilliant autumn colours in the landscape, or the passage of the full moon as it travels across the sky. In these 'me-time' moments we are allowing a sense of calm and tranquility wash over us as we marvel at the pillars of flame of the larches, or seeing the full moon through the branches of a tree.

Our mind might be clear of all conscious thought but there is something else going on in our subconscious ... Reflection is an interpretation of what is going on between learning and thinking; it is meant to stimulate our intellect *and* intuition. It may confound, or it may provide one of those '*Aha!*' moments. Reflections are thoughts or ideas that occur as a result of this 'me-time', which then become a subject for serious thought or consideration for a period of time in our daily life.

The Wild Larder

True gourmets are learning that, if they want to expand their repertoire, wild food is the way forward and wild food takes some beating. Elizabeth David in *An Omelette and a Glass of Wine* tells us:

> 'Pale apricot-coloured chanterelle mushrooms from sodden Surrey woods have only to be washed and washed and washed until all the grit has gone, every scrap, and cooked instantly before the bloom and that extraordinary, delicate, almost flower-like scent have faded'.

There are so many wild foods available at this time of year in terms of nuts, fruit and fungi, although the latter shouldn't be picked unless we're absolutely sure of what we're gathering. An interesting point to bear in mind is that fungi, once considered plant-like organisms, are actually more closely related to animals than plants. As it turns out, animals and fungi share a common ancestor and branched away from plants at some point about 1.1 billion years ago. It was only later that animals and fungi separated on the genealogical tree of life, making mushrooms more closely related to humans than plants. So, I guess that takes them off the vegetarian/vegan menu!

One of the richest bounties of autumn is having to wait for the first frost before picking sloes from the blackthorn to make our annual supply of sloe gin – a witch's own home-made rescue remedy – and sloes are plentiful along roadsides. We just have to remember where we saw those all beautiful white flowers in the early spring ...

Recipe: Traditional Sloe Gin

Half fill clean, dry wine bottles with the fruit previously pricked with a darning needle. An old-fashioned recipe says to add to each 1oz crushed barley sugar, 2-3 drops of almond essence. Fill the bottles with dry, unsweetened gin, cork them securely, and allow them to remain in a moderately warm place for 3 months. At the end of this time, strain the liqueur through fine muslin until quite clear, then bottle. Cork securely and store away in a cool, dry place until required for use. There are regional differences in the preparation of sloe gin, with modern recipes replacing the barley sugar and almond essence with 4ozs of granulated sugar. [*Traditional Witchcraft for Fields and Hedgerows*]

Chapter Five

Winter – the Path of Mid-Winter

According to the astronomical definition of the seasons, the Winter Solstice also marks the beginning of winter, which lasts until the Vernal Equinox (20th or 21st March in the Northern Hemisphere, or 22nd or 23rd September in the Southern Hemisphere).

> On a frosty day in mid-winter a sinister beauty etches the land, embalming it in a hard glaze of ice. Although many of the plants have set seed and withered, and many animals have migrated or are in hibernation, there is still a surprising amount of activity in the countryside, especially on milder days when the sun is shining. [*The Four Seasons*]

The winter months are often thought of as the drab time of the year. The colourful berries and fruits of autumn have either been eaten or have become dry and shrivelled, while leafless trees and dead vegetation contribute to the starkness of the field and urban woodland. And yet ... along **The Path** there are still jewels to be found before the weak summer sun destroys these wonders. Overnight ice crystals have formed on the teasles and dead flower-heads of the Umbellifers (wild carrot, cow parsley, etc.), making even solitary specimens a spectacular sight. Or further along by the plank bridge, preserved under a covering of frost and snow, the seed-heads of the bulrush start to lose their velvet smoothness as the tightly packed seeds get ready to be dispersed by the wind.

As vegetation recedes along the edges of *The Path*, the bare verges are stripped down to the bare stones that often appear to have a life of their own. Stones have long been said to be the bare bones of the Earth and this myth *does* give stones a life, lifting them from Ice Age graves into sunlight to become the bane of 21st-century gardeners. Taking a leaf out of Chet Raymo's book, *Honey from Stone*, it's time to discover something else to make us think about our daily walk on a much deeper level.

Winter is the time when stones get up and go, heaving themselves into animation, shaking off the stillness of summer hibernation. They burgeon underfoot like cabbages, shouldering aside the frozen earth. There is a reason for this winter mobility and it's called frost heaving, caused by alternate cycles of freezing and thawing. The soil surrounding a buried stone freezes and expands, lifting the stone and creating a cavity underneath. Pebbles or grit sift into the cavity and when the ground thaws, the stone is prevented from settling back into its old place It has been lifted, ever so slightly. Another freeze, another thaw; the cycle is repeated. Millimetre by millimetre the stone makes its way to the surface, finally pushing against tree roots, meadow vegetation, asphalt or any other obstruction that blocks its ponderous resurrection …

And how often do we find our attention caught by a small pebble because of its colour or shape that has suddenly appeared on *The Path* or in the stream bed? We cannot resist the urge to pick it up and take it home where it joins others of its kind in a large glass bowl; or we keep it in the pocket of our dog-walking coat where it acts as a 'worry stone' as we follow our daily routine. The concept of a worry stone began by the simple action of picking up a smooth stone or pebble and fiddling with it for relaxation or anxiety relief. The smoothness of the stone is most often created naturally by running water and the action of moving one's thumb back and forth across the stone can reduce stress quite significantly. And we really *don't* need to pay silly money for on-line versions that can be picked up from anywhere: the gravel by a park bench, fresh from the earth on our daily walk; those that mysteriously appear on **The Path** from nowhere …

As the days grow shorter, we might be tempted to explore the canal tow-paths that run through our towns or villages. Although the Romans dug Britain's first canal – the Fossdyke – the great time for canal construction occurred during the 18-19th centuries for the transportation of freight between the mining, industrial and commercial centers of the country. Today commercial traffic is almost non-existent but its place has been taken by a massive upsurge in recreational use – not only allowing the larger canals to be kept open, but also enabling sections of disused ones to be brought back to a working state. And yet, as Richard Mabey remarks in *The Unofficial Countryside*:

> In a stretch of canal near my home there was a steel narrow-boat moored for most of the spring and summer. It had been used for dredging and was full of a tangled mass of silt, beer cans and bank-side vegetation. No one seemed concerned about moving it and by mid-summer it was like a floating window-box, sprouting sharp green blades of yellow iris and great water grass, bur-marigold and the pink flower-spikes of redleg …

Where a canal tow-path is no longer in constant use and under wear from the tramp of walkers and anglers, plants like the stately yellow-flag can become quickly established. As the water level falls, the marginal vegetation extends outwards from the banks and the central channel comes narrower and shallower. If the mileage of canals still in working use was added to those that have been abandoned, there would be a wild-life corridor some 3000 miles long stretching the length and breadth of the country.

On the surface, in winter tow-paths can look as dull and uninteresting as the water because the changes that occur along a working canal, however, are slight; navigation channels must be kept open, banks maintained, depth kept constant by periodic dredging and towpaths cleared. All along the 'cut' the fauna is adapting to the new season and the changing habitat. Therefore, a walk along the tow-path today is likely to produce the same bird species, mammals and flowers that we would have seen a century or two ago. The only things missing are the horse-drawn boats.

Here, the woods and adjoining land looks bleak and empty in winter, there is constant activity in the thorny hedgerow thickets along *The Path*. Hedgerows, particularly of hawthorn with its tangle of spiny twigs were planted primarily to contain livestock and to offer them shelter from bad weather. Wildlife benefits in winter since many birds' roost in hedges overnight and a dense hedge offers them protection from ground predators and also from the wind which causes the greatest loss of heat and energy during the long winter nights. With the onset of winter, many insects also seek nooks and crannies in the interior of the hedge to hibernate. And when walking past don't be deceive by the bare twigs – there is as much activity in a hawthorn hedge as in a high-rise block of flats!

Another observation of Richard Mabey's is that to a well-wrapped human with a fire and a hot meal to return to, there is something very up-lifting about a walk on a bright winter's day. The landscape seems stripped clean, pared back for the fight against the cold …

But for the creatures that live there, the fight is a real life and death struggle. It is then that the urban areas, with their warmer air, unfrozen water and food parcels handed out by kindly humans, become a real blessing. I could not count the number of times I have strode manfully out on winter says into an almost birdless landscape in the deep countryside, only to return and finds the belt of bijou gardens I had left hours before brimming with birds. It's been estimated that during the terrible freeze-ups, over a million birds are saved from starvation by the food provided by householders ...

But the food that is both deliberately an unintentionally provided in gardens doesn't just benefit the birds. The house-holder gets their reward too, in the shape of closer and more intimate views of birds of greater numbers of more species than at any other time of the year. They are tamer, too – or at least more prepared to suspend their suspicion of humans – and we can watch these processes of adjustments actually taking place.

And while on the subject of fauna, I recently read an article by writer and research fellow at Yale University, in which he commented that having a dog encourages you to enter into an environment in a more attentive way. 'There is something about being around an animal. They have this great propensity to focus on one thing, and the rest of the world falls away from them. I aspire to do some human version of that'. This is because dogs have the ability to open up the world around us. They attract the attention of like-minded people because dogs are very sociable creatures ... and their contribution to humans as assistance, rescue and security dogs is immeasurable ... since they also act as a deterrent against unwanted attention.

If you don't have a dog of your own then why not offer to walk a neighbour's while they're out at work? A dog will introduce you to many of the different aspects of the natural world you never even knew existed. Dogs are very curious creatures who have no qualms about sticking their noses into anything and everything. A dog's curiosity is most likely compounded by the fact that they have a very strong sense of smell and sight, and can pick up on things than humans cannot, such as minute smells and very high and very low-pitched sounds. Because of this, a dog might be curious about something that a human doesn't even realize is close by.

Unlike most humans, dogs feel an urge to explore and to gain information about the world around them ... and if something is new, a dog is very likely to try to figure out what the thing is. They will push limits until they realize that something is harmful or uninteresting ... and we quickly find that *their* curiosity is contagious because they encourage us to 'stand and stare' while they tiffle about in the undergrowth.

Walking out in the company of a dog gives us an added sense of purpose; a ready-made companion with whom we can discuss the current political situation, global warming, or the economic up/down turn without censure or ridicule. Dogs provide a shoulder to cry on, or make us laugh out loud at their antics; dogs introduce us to *their* natural world which is often a lot less stressful and a lot more meaningful than our own. They keep us out for longer, and we walk further and a lot more slowly than when we were walking alone.

Dogs play their part in our cultural heritage and in different traditions ghostly hounds are found, e.g. Gabriel Hounds (England), Ratchets (England), Yell Hounds (Isle of Man), related to Herne the Hunter's hounds, which form part of the Wild Hunt. Similar hounds occur in Devon - particularly on Dartmoor and Cornwall but it is not clear whether they stem from Brythonic or Saxon origins. In Wales, the Cŵn Annwn were associated with migrating geese, supposedly because the birds' honking in the night is reminiscent of barking dogs.

And we are reminded of these old stories as the sun starts to set and the honking chorus of Canada Geese breaks the tranquility of the winter afternoon. First introduced as an ornamental bird on lakes, a considerable number of them became wild. Canada Geese are sociable and noisy birds that live near fresh water areas such as lakes and ponds which are often near urban and city parks with large numbers roosting together in the autumn and winter on mud banks. Canada Geese are by nature migratory but those living in the UK and Ireland tend to be resident birds, with some wintering from Scandinavia join resident birds in the UK and Ireland in the autumn. They are distinguished by flying in a neat 'V' formation during long distance migration.

There is a chill in the air as our spinning planet leans into its winter curve away from the sun and another flight of geese high above the tree tops catches the last direct rays before going to their roosts at dusk. As the light changes our canine companion tells us that it's time to go home and share hot buttered crumpets in front of a roaring fire!

A winter fire-symbol is, of course, the Furze, Gorse or Win - a thorny plant often viewed as having protective powers. The flowers are a deep yellow and have a pungent coconut scent. Although the main flowering period is from March to August, flowers can be found on bushes throughout the year. There are three species of furze, which all have slightly different flowering seasons, so that to the casual observer it would appear that the bush is almost always in bloom. This lengthy flowering led to the country saying: 'When the gorse is out of blossom, kissing is out of fashion'. The habit of adding a sprig of furze bloom in a bridal bouquet was thought to allude to this, the all-year-round blossom being a symbol of continuous fertility.

Popular with bakers to whom it was sold as fuel for their ovens. It has a high concentration of oil in its leaves and branches, and so catches fire easily and burns well, giving off a heat almost equal to that of charcoal. Older plants can carry a lot of dead wood, so furze can be a hazard in hot, dry summers. Furze can also be used as fodder for animals. It was said that an acre of furze could provide enough winter feed for six horses. It has half the protein content of oats. Horses and goats can strip the leaves and eat them straight from the plant, but it was usual practice to run the branches through stone mills or hit them with wooden mallets. This crushed the thorns and reduced the wood to a moss like consistency, which made it more palatable, especially to cows and sheep. The bushes were often deliberately burnt down in order to encourage new growth, the fresh sprouts of furze and grass providing easily accessible food for stock.

The bark and flowers produce a fine yellow dye. In Ireland the flowers were also used to flavour and add colour to whiskey and the Vikings were reputed to use them to make beer. They can also be used to make wine and tea. Studies in the 19th-century confirmed that the high alkaline content of the plant had a purgative effect. An infusion of the blooms, as a drink, was given to children suffering from scarlet fever. It was also used to cleanse the home; '... against fleas, take this same wort, with its seed sodden; sprinkle it into the house; it killeth the fleas'. In homeopathy furze is used to help people who have given up hope, who have no faith in the future. It puts people in touch with their own inner resources and helps them move forward by releasing courage and determination.

As one of the sacred trees, furze was included in the Celtic Beltane bonfires. The stock would be herded between these for purification and protection before being released onto the summer grazing. When this tradition diminished, torches of furze were still carried around the herds and farm buildings in order to cleanse the air and protect the animals against sterility. Furze is closely associated with the sun god Lugh, the Celtic god of light and genius and with the Spring Equinox, at which time it's one of the only plants in full flower, although folklore attaches it to festivals throughout the spring and summer months as a symbol of the power of the sun. In Brittany the Celtic festival of Lughnasdagh, on August 1st, is known as The Festival of Golden Gorse.

As an evergreen that flowers the whole year round, furze is seen to carry within it a spark of the sun's life-giving energy, a spark that can be seen even through the darker winter months. It is a symbol of encouragement and a promise of good things to come. Furze tells us to remain focused and optimistic, even in the darkest days. To keep hopeful and remain constant throughout the inevitable periods of difficulty we all experience. As one of the first spring flowering plants, the furze provides a plentiful supply of pollen for bees when they first come out of hibernation. The product of the bees' labour – honey - is the Celtic symbol of wisdom, achieved through hard work and dedication. The furze tells us that if we apply ourselves and keep faith in the future, we will be rewarded. However bleak things may appear to be there is always the possibility of periods of fertility, creativity and well-being; whilst its thorns remind us that there is protection from unwanted ideas or influences.

Just as evergreen furze brightens up the field margin, so the Holly and Ivy add colour to the winter woodland, coupled together in the ancient Yuletide carol, *The Holly and the Ivy*. From **The Path** we can take one of the lesser trodden paths that take us passed the holly thicket deep in the heart of the wood. Even in mid-winter when the surrounding trees have been stripped bare of leaves, this is the darkest part of the wood because the holly canopy is so dense that sunlight never reaches the woodland floor where the ground is carpeted with the dried, spiky leaves. Here there is a sense of magic and mystery that suggests why this is a path lessen trodden for in the grey days of winter the deep shadows beneath the trees are silent and brooding.

In the older part of the wood, many of the trees are cloaked in ivy. Like many other evergreens, ivy symbolises the concept of eternity; a belief in everlasting life and resurrection after death. Because it is often found growing on dead and decayed trees, it came to represent the immortal soul –which lives on even after the body has returned to the earth. Yet at the same time, because it was often found in sites of death (including cemeteries and old tombstones) it was also viewed as an emblem of mortality.

Like the holly, the ivy is also one of the plants found in the Celtic Tree Calendar, where it is known as Gort, and the botany of the plant has clearly influenced its symbolism: amongst its various meanings, ivy represents connections and friendships, undoubtedly influenced by the plant's natural tendency to weave and intertwine during growth. Such connections often play an important role in our celebrations as we reach out to family and friends, to recall cherished memories and create new ones, especially around the time of the Mid-Winter Festival and Yule.

Ivy grows well throughout the UK and can be found in many habitats including woodland, scrub, wasteland and on isolated trees. It is tolerant of shade and survives in all but the most dry, waterlogged or acidic soils. It flowers from September to November and fruits ripen in November to January; its nectar, pollen and berries of ivy are an essential food source for insects and birds during autumn and winter when food is scarce. It also provides shelter for insects, birds, bats and other small mammals. The high fat content of the berries is a nutritious food resource for birds and they are eaten by a range of species including thrushes, blackcaps, woodpigeons and blackbirds.

By the plank bridge the community allotments are winding down for the winter. Late season crops are still to be harvested but by and large the individual plots are bare soil between the wooden sheds and the closed-up greenhouses. But this seasonal bareness may tempt us to start off own therapeutic attempts at growing plants we can utilize in the kitchen. Those of us lucky enough to have even a small urban garden will recognize the restorative powers of its atmosphere, whether we are simply relaxing in it, or working to maintain it. Gardening therapy is becoming more and more popular but even if we don't have a garden, we can garden on a smaller scale by growing some plants in pots on a balcony, or perhaps a few window boxes with ornamental plants or herbs. Spending time with plants really can improve our health and well-being.

Now is also a good time to collect ash sticks for the 'ashen faggot' – and old English Yuletide tradition similar to that of the Yule log and related to the Wassail tradition, since burning ash wood at Yule was said to bring prosperity. A faggot is a large bundle of ash sticks bound with nine green lengths of ash bands or 'beams, preferably all from the same tree. At an appropriate moment during Christmas Eve when all the family is gathered together, the faggot is burned in the hearth while people watching sing carols by candlelight.

The wassail party passes around the bundle of ash sticks, twigs or branches – containing the remnant of the previous year's faggot - bound with green ash withies, which is then placed onto the fire. It is done traditionally by the oldest person in the room and the heat created is a symbolic comfort in mid-winter nights. As each binding bursts, the watchers toast it with a drink. When the bindings have all burst and the bundle has fallen loose, the person who plans to host the festivities next year takes one of the half-burned ash sticks and saves it until the following Yule, when it will go in the centre of their own ashen faggot. This tradition symbolizes continuity of life. Since today's fireplaces aren't usually large enough to burn a good-sized ashen faggot, we can utilize the patio log burner or fire pit; although we can make half a dozen miniature faggots to suit an indoor hearth.

Wassailing is a very ancient custom that is rarely observed today. The word 'wassail' comes from the Anglo-Saxon phrase *waes hael*, which means good health. Originally, the wassail was a drink made of mulled ale, curdled cream, roasted apples, eggs, cloves, ginger, nutmeg and sugar. It was served from huge bowls, often made of silver or pewter. Jesus College, in Oxford University, has a Wassail bowl that can hold ten gallons! The wassail drink mixture was sometimes called 'lamb's wool', because of the pulp of the roasted apples looked all frothy and a bit like … lambs wool.

Wassailing was traditionally done on New Year's Eve or old Twelfth Night (17th January), but the wealthy drank wassail on all Twelve days of Christmas. In parts of England (such as Somerset and Sussex) where apples are grown, especially for cider, wassailing still takes place on Twelfth Night (or sometimes New Year's Eve, or even Christmas Eve). People go into apple orchards and then sing songs, make loud noises and dance around to scare of any evil spirits and also to 'wake up' the trees so they will give a good crop!

If, however, we feel ourselves in a more contemplative frame of mind ... on the last day of the year, 'whose midnight I habitually devote to a meditation on the past, culminating in the formulation of the future' as Aleister Crowley wrote We might just find that all those daily wanderings and musings while walking *The Path* have culminated in the thought that while we seek the deeply hidden essence of creation, we are, by and large, content that much of what we seek remains unknown. Nevertheless, *we shall not cease from our exploration* and to paraphrase the old Irish blessing, originally written in Gaelicas May the road rise to meet you is actually mistranslated quite a bit from the original language it was written in. 'Rise' actually translates more accurately to 'succeed'. So ... *May The Path rise to meet you* ...

Exercise: A Sense of Deliberation

Deliberation is a process of thoughtfully weighing options prior to making decisions with varying amounts of information. If we work in an office or building with bright lights then we need to inject some daylight into our lives. Daylight and Nature help to keep our immunity and circadian rhythm in balance. So, let's get outside during our break time ...

Once we jump on the wellness band-wagon, however, we quickly run the risk of becoming a Wellness-Bore on the subject of the life-enhancing properties of our new awareness routine. Or as columnist Sophie White commented recently: 'You can't swing a dead cat these days without someone trying to revive it with their meditation practice, their mindfulness, or probiotics'.

The whole point of the exercise is to find a *simple* method of soothing away the stresses of the day. And joining in a girl's nights in/out conversations about the latest mental/physical health fad will not work its magic if it becomes a competitive conversation stopper. There is nothing more tedious than being subjected to other people's endorsements for diets, meditation, yoga classes, exercise routines, etc., because listening to the wellness plans of others is about as interesting as listening to them recounting their experience of colonic irrigation and just about as passé ...

Our own *personal* remedies should remain just that and one of the most important is our intake of vitamin D – because if we shun the sun, suffer from milk allergies, or adhere to a strict vegan diet, we may be at risk of vitamin D deficiency. Known as the sunshine vitamin, vitamin D is produced by the body in response to skin being exposed to sunlight but do bear in mind that as we get older, our skin has a harder time producing vitamin D.

Our body creates vitamin D from *direct* sunlight on our skin when we're outdoors. From about late March/early April to the end of September, most of us should be able to get all the vitamin D we need from sunlight by being out in the sun daily for short periods with our forearms, hands or lower legs uncovered. In the UK, winter sunlight doesn't contain enough UVB radiation (October to early March) for our skin to be able to make vitamin D., so during these months we rely on getting our vitamin D from food sources (including fortified foods) and supplements.

The fact that something is ordinary, traditional, or natural, and not complicated seems to go against the grain of contemporary thought but, hey ... what's there not to like about it?

The Wild Larder

Wild foods require none of the attention demanded by garden plants, and possess the added attraction of having to be found. I think I would rate this as perhaps the most attractive single feature of wild food use [*Food for Free*]

Rosehips (*Rosa canina*) provide a splash of vivid colour in the winter hedgerows when all the other leaves have been stripped away. Rosehips have been used as a food for centuries and there is an often-quoted recipe dating from 1730 for a 'rosehip dessert'. It was not until World War II, however, they were sourced on a grand scale because the wild fruit was found to contain twenty-times the amount of vitamin C in oranges. The Ministry of Food recipe (1943) in *Hedgrerow Harvest* is still widely quoted for use to this day. Rosehips can be carried for general good luck or strung like beads for luck in love; or used as offerings to encourage friendly spirits to take up residence. [*Wort Lore: The Craft of Witches*]

Recipe: Rosehip Syrup

For rosehip syrup, you'll need about 2lb of ripe fruit and 1lb of sugar. Cover the hips with water, boil for ten minutes, mash and strain. Add the sugar, boil again for five minutes and bottle. Including the same number of apples produces a pleasant 'honey'. A 16th century recipe adds sugar, cinnamon, ginger and lemon juice to the stewed fruit to make a puree for tarts and toppings. Make sure you extract all the prickly seeds, as these can be a dangerous internal irritant. [*Traditional Witchcraft for Fields and Hedgerows*]

The Path of Mindfulness

Once we make a conscious effort to step onto the pagan path, we find that everything combines to achieve a calm mental state by focusing our awareness on the present moment, while calmly acknowledging and accepting our feelings, thoughts, and bodily sensations in order to develop as overall sense of Wellness. For example:

Well-Being: Here we are looking at physical fitness as a state of health and well-being and, more specifically, the ability to perform aspects of sports, occupations and daily activities because physical fitness is generally achieved through proper nutrition, a regular programme of moderate exercise, and regular good night's sleep. Physical activity boosts the immune system and achieving resilience through physical fitness promotes a vast and complex range of health-related benefits. Individuals who keep up physical fitness levels generally regulate their distribution of body fat and stay away from obesity.

Well-fed: The phrase 'You Are What You Eat' means that it is important to eat *good* food in order to be healthy and fit. The first mention of the phrase came from the 1826 work *Physiologie du Gout, ou Medetations de Gastronomie Transcendante,* in which French author Anthelme Brillat-Savarin wrote: "Tell me what you eat and I will tell you what you are." Brillat-Savarin was a physician and father of the Paleo and low-carb diets.

The nutritional content of what we eat determines the composition of our cell membranes, bone marrow, blood, hormones, tissue, organs, skin, and hair. And for all the food-fads perhaps we should take a moment to reflect that a recent study shows our great-grandparent's diet holds the key to better health today, simply because modern eating habits have led to a decline in types of healthy bacteria which protect the immune system.

Eating well is part of the strategy that can reduce the risk of any chronic disease and even improve the condition of our very genes as Hippocrates (400BC) is alleged to have observed: 'Let thy food be thy medicine and medicine be thy food', and often used to emphasize the importance of nutrition to prevent or cure disease.

Well-Balanced: Physical activity can also improve psychological and emotional well-being due to an increase in blood flow to the brain and the release of hormones. Being out and about and taking the time to stand and stare also promotes our spiritual wellness - that personal viewpoint involving values and beliefs, while mental activities optimize brain matter and create well-being. GPs are apparently now issuing 'park prescriptions' to encourage patients to get out more and use local parks and green-spaces to reduce blood-pressure, stress and obesity levels.

Spiritual well-being, of course, means the ability to experience and integrate meaning and purpose into life through our connectedness with self, others, art, music, literature, nature, or a power greater than ourselves ... which, in turn, leads to a sense of well-balanced spirituality in harmony with our surroundings. For example: the Earth has natural electromagnetic waves, so when we stand barefoot on the ground – sand, grass, soil, or gravel are conductive surfaces – and energy exchange occurs. If we think of ourselves as a battery and over time our 'battery' loses power then we need to recharge ourselves with negatively-charged electrons from the Earth. These neutralise the free radicals that cause inflammation and disease. Standing barefoot on the ground for as little as four-minutes a day can help.

Well-informed: Nature is being destroyed at a rate hundreds of times higher than any time in the past decade, all as a result of human activity. Dr James Lovelock, who formed his 'Gaia Hypothesis' back in the 1960s, is now warning that global warming has passed the tipping point and that the various so-called green activities and life-style adjustments to help the environment are a waste of time. Humans cannot save themselves by going back to nature, says the climate scientist, who believes that in 100-years' time, 80% of the population will be gone and that those remaining will have developed an understanding of the Earth and how to live with it!

It's a frightening thought but in reality, *The Path* begins and ends at our own front door. And we may think we know the world, because we follow the diktats of current life-style gurus but we have lost the knowledge of the special things in life, *because we have stopped looking for them*. Often a witch may find that a long abstinence from magical practices has injured their powers but once they resume their elementary drill of walking *The Path*, they soon get back their old form, instead of having to climb the ladder again from the bottom.

So … forget the diet fads, fitness fashions and life-style gurus, and reconnect with the earth by the simplest means possible by interacting with it. *The Path* is about following basic paganism in its purest form and restoring the link to the 'magical memory'. Because all memory is a re-awakening of ancient impressions; allowing us to penetrate to the deeper layers of our unconscious self from where events in the past sometimes throw light on the present. Hopefully these simple exercises have put you in the right frame of mind to approach a pagan life-style with a receptive frame of mind for these are just the first baby-steps on *The Path*.

It may also have come as a surprise that there are no complicated routines and customs to help you tune in to the voices along *The Path*, but as gardener Monty Don commented recently:

> 'You can always make an emotional connection to beauty even if you don't understand what the beauty is or why you feel the way you do. Emotion will bubble to the surface from some source, even though you can't put your finger on that source.'

And it *is* possible to be intensely spiritual without being religious for as Chet Raymo writes: *When God is Gone Everything is Holy*. For when we talk about the folklore of a people or culture, we are referring to the whole body of traditional beliefs, customs, and stories of a community, passed through the generations by word of mouth. When writing about the sculpture *Nature Unveiling Herself to Science* Raymo observes:

> Meanwhile, there she stands, on her pedestal in the Musee d'Orsay, taunting our curiosity – the bared breasts, the glimpse of toes – still after millennia of scientific discovery, wrapped in mystery. She does indeed love to hide, this enigmatic goddess ... and I suspect that another two-and-a-half millennia from now we'll still be wondering what she has yet to reveal.

What people have thought, all over the world and all through history, about their folk traditions *is* important not only for what it may tell us about their perspective of life and death as the ancients viewed it, but for what it tells us about humankind today. *If nothing else, it shows what we have lost!*

Nevertheless, the current trend of what Professor Raymo terms as going at religion 'like B-movie slashers armed with Ockham's razor' until all that's left are the gory shreds of miracles and superstitions. I agree with Raymo that God had it coming but like him I also feel there is something amiss with this militant, slash-and-burn atheism. Instead the good Professor switches metaphors and turns the new one on its ear in suggesting that God's detractors throw out the bath water with the baby ...

> In my inverted cliché, let 'bath water' stand for the mind-stretching, jaw-dropping, in-your-face wonder of the universe itself, the Heraclitan mystery that hides in every rainbow, every snowflake, every living cell. After all, water, as much as anything in our environment, is an adequate symbol for the creative agency that forges atoms in the hot interiors of stars, weds oxygen to hydrogen, and wets the Earth with the stuff of life and consciousness – an agency worthy of attention, reverence, thanksgiving, praise.
>
> As for 'the baby', let that represent the cultural accretions that religious traditions have affixed to the 'water' of mystery – the anthropomorphisms, misplaced pieties, triumphalism, intolerance towards 'infidels', supposed miracles, and supernatural imaginings. Memes without substance. So, yes, toss out the baby, but save the water.

Similarly, currently just over half of the world's multi-cultural population lives in urban area and this is expected to reach two-thirds by 2050. And this is why governments are looking at ways of using Nature to help making cities sustainable and healthy places in which to live and work. City planners are becoming more aware of the importance of access to natural spaces, and there are many projects aimed at transforming once-derelict city spaces into green oases. We only need to glance at a city park on a fine day to see how much people appreciate these green spaces to sit and eat their lunch, take a break or go for some exercise. It makes sense to the ordinary man and woman 'but now scientific evidence is helping to make a case for the importance of including nature in urban planning, for both the mental and physical health of the residents', says Professor Miyazaki.

Most urban areas *do* have pockets of Nature, whether it's a local park, an area of waste ground, or an overgrown path along the side of a canal – even an old churchyard. Any space where there are plants growing can offer relaxation effects to those who are prepared to seek them out and spend time there. Unfortunately, many of us are simply too busy to put aside time for ourselves – giving our minds and bodies no chance to unwind and disperse the stress that comes from being in such close proximity to our fellow humans. Which, in itself, is a recipe for disaster.

I believe simplicity is the key and is the central principle of my personal teaching is to compel a pupil to rely on their own resources, and having acquired good judgement and confidence, to develop intelligent initiative. A good teacher *must* be able to show their pupils how to choose the best hand-holds and foot-holds, but not let them acquire the habit of looking for the teacher to tell them what to do at every turn. Or to quote Albert Einstein: 'I never teach my pupils, I only attempt to provide the conditions in which they can learn'.

Or Bob Clay-Egerton, who taught me how to teach:

Suggestions are made in order to give rise to thought. Not standard items of belief, they are simply intended to *provoke thought*. The pupil has the brain stimulated in a way that does not easily occur where training involves spoon-feeding with 'what must be believed'. Understanding has to be worked for ... but questions *can* be asked ... and the answers may give rise to totally different possible answers. No matter! The member thinks for themselves. They are responsible for their own progress on their own individual path.

So ... let's take a leaf out of the urban pagan's handbook book and keep silence about those special 'me-time' routines that works for you and embrace the thought that when we are walking along *The Path*, we are living in the portal between knowledge and mystery, between the commonplace and the divine. And life becomes so much simpler as a result.

Sources & Bibliography

The Country Book of the Year, Dennis L Furnell (David & Charles)

The Flowering of Britain, Richard Mabey (Hutchinson)

Observing with the Twelve Senses, Tom van Gelder (Louis Bolk Instituut)

The Patchwork Landscape, ed Euan Dunn (Readers Digest)

The Path, Chet Raymo (Walker)

The Physiology of Taste or, Transcendental Gastronomy, Jean Anthelme Brillat-Savarin (Merchant Books)

Traditional Witchcraft for Urban Living, Melusine Draco (Moon Books)

Traditional Witchcraft for Field & Hedgerows, Melusine Draco (Moon Books)

Traditional Witchcraft and the Path to the Mysteries, Melusine Draco (Moon Books)

The Unofficial Countryside, Richard Mabey (Collins)

When God is Gone Everything is Holy, Chet Raymo (Sorin Books)

Western Animism: Zen and the Art of Practical Paganism, Melusine Draco (Moon Books)

Wild Flowers of Britain, Roger Phillips (Pan)

Wild Food, Jane Eastoe (National Trust)

Wild Life on Your Doorstep, ed. Rober Gibbons (Readers Digest)

Wort-Lore: The Craft of Witches, Melusine Draco (Ignotus)

**MOON
BOOKS**

PAGANISM & SHAMANISM

What is Paganism? A religion, a spirituality, an alternative belief system, nature worship? You can find support for all these definitions (and many more) in dictionaries, encyclopaedias, and text books of religion, but subscribe to any one and the truth will evade you. Above all Paganism is a creative pursuit, an encounter with reality, an exploration of meaning and an expression of the soul. Druids, Heathens, Wiccans and others, all contribute their insights and literary riches to the Pagan tradition. Moon Books invites you to begin or to deepen your own encounter, right here, right now.

If you have enjoyed this book, why not tell other readers by posting a review on your preferred book site.

Recent bestsellers from Moon Books are:

Journey to the Dark Goddess
How to Return to Your Soul
Jane Meredith
Discover the powerful secrets of the Dark Goddess and transform your depression, grief and pain into healing and integration.
Paperback: 978-1-84694-677-6 ebook: 978-1-78099-223-5

Shamanic Reiki
Expanded Ways of Working with Universal Life Force Energy
Llyn Roberts, Robert Levy
Shamanism and Reiki are each powerful ways of healing; together, their power multiplies. *Shamanic Reiki* introduces techniques to help healers and Reiki practitioners tap ancient healing wisdom.
Paperback: 978-1-84694-037-8 ebook: 978-1-84694-650-9

Pagan Portals – The Awen Alone
Walking the Path of the Solitary Druid
Joanna van der Hoeven
An introductory guide for the solitary Druid, *The Awen Alone* will accompany you as you explore, and seek out your own place within the natural world.
Paperback: 978-1-78279-547-6 ebook: 978-1-78279-546-9

A Kitchen Witch's World of Magical Herbs & Plants
Rachel Patterson
A journey into the magical world of herbs and plants, filled with magical uses, folklore, history and practical magic. By popular writer, blogger and kitchen witch, Tansy Firedragon.
Paperback: 978-1-78279-621-3 ebook: 978-1-78279-620-6

Medicine for the Soul
The Complete Book of Shamanic Healing
Ross Heaven
All you will ever need to know about shamanic healing and how to become your own shaman…
Paperback: 978-1-78099-419-2 ebook: 978-1-78099-420-8

Shaman Pathways – The Druid Shaman
Exploring the Celtic Otherworld
Danu Forest
A practical guide to Celtic shamanism with exercises and techniques as well as traditional lore for exploring the Celtic Otherworld.
Paperback: 978-1-78099-615-8 ebook: 978-1-78099-616-5

Traditional Witchcraft for the Woods and Forests
A Witch's Guide to the Woodland with Guided Meditations and
Pathworking
Mélusine Draco
A Witch's guide to walking alone in the woods, with guided
meditations and pathworking.
Paperback: 978-1-84694-803-9 ebook: 978-1-84694-804-6

Naming the Goddess
Trevor Greenfield
Naming the Goddess is written by over eighty adherents and
scholars of Goddess and Goddess Spirituality.
Paperback: 978-1-78279-476-9 ebook: 978-1-78279-475-2

Shapeshifting into Higher Consciousness
Heal and Transform Yourself and Our World with Ancient
Shamanic and Modern Methods
Llyn Roberts
Ancient and modern methods that you can use every day to
transform yourself and make a positive difference in the world.
Paperback: 978-1-84694-843-5 ebook: 978-1-84694-844-2

Readers of ebooks can buy or view any of these bestsellers by
clicking on the live link in the title. Most titles are published in
paperback and as an ebook. Paperbacks are available in traditional
bookshops. Both print and ebook formats are available online.

Find more titles and sign up to our readers' newsletter at
http://www.johnhuntpublishing.com/paganism
Follow us on Facebook at https://www.facebook.com/MoonBooks
and Twitter at https://twitter.com/MoonBooksJHP